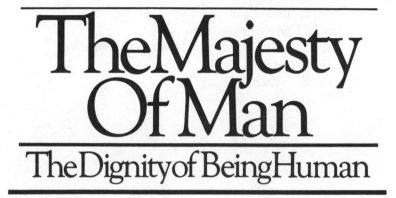

The Majesty Of Man

The Dignity of Being Human

RONALD B. ALLEN

MULTNOMAH

Portland, Oregon 97266

Other books by Ronald B. Allen:
Praise! A Matter of Life and Breath
Worship: Rediscovering the Missing Jewel
    (with Gordon Borror)
Praise: The Response to All of Life
When Song Is New: Understanding the Kingdom
    in the Psalms
Abortion: When Does Life Begin?

Unless otherwise indicated, Scripture quotations are from the Holy Bible: New International Version, © 1978 by the International Bible Society. Used by permission of Zondervan Bible Publishers.

Edited by Rod Morris
Cover design and illustration by Britt Taylor Collins

THE MAJESTY OF MAN
© 1984 by Multnomah Press
Portland, Oregon 97266

Printed in the United States of America

Library of Congress Cataloging in Publication Data

Allen, Ronald Barclay.
    The majesty of man.

    Bibliography: p. 207
    Includes index.
    1. Man (Christian theology)   2. Bible. O.T. Psalms VIII—Criticism,
interpretation, etc.   I. Title.
BT701.2.A45   1984   233   84-984
ISBN 0-88070-065-3

88   89   90   91   92   93   –   10   9   8   7   6   5   4   3   2

To our children,
Laureen, Craig, Bruce, Rachel—
May each of you discover your true
humanity in the Savior Y'shua.

Contents

Acknowledgments

I so appreciate the editorial staff at Multnomah Press who believed in this project before I did. Julie Cave saw in this idea more than a booklet; Rod Morris saw in this idea something of a book.

I also appreciate Adam Osborne and the machine he has made which helped me to write a book in praise of man (*'adam*). If his company were to be reorganized, I have a great name for it: Osborne-again. I hope so!

Acknowledgment is gratefully made to Augsburg Publishing House for permission to quote from *Bible Readings for Couples* by Margaret and Erling Wold, © 1980.

Introduction

The most pressing theological question of our day is the same one raised by David the psalmist over three thousand years ago. But it keeps on pressing:

WHAT IS MAN?

In the present decade this old question is beset with new imperatives. In newsmagazines, daily papers, internal company communications, and especially in the public broadcast media, we are confronted with the question over and over again. Some of the new issues are:

• New genetics involve in vitro fertilization and ovum transfer. Here we find our shared delight with new parents is troubled by questions of ethics, law, and genetic manipulation. We ask, What is man?

• Abortion on demand has led to the deaths of millions of unborn babies over the last decade. It is not a long step from active abortion of fetal life to passive killing of full-term babies whose conditions do not meet the expectations of the parents. "Baby Doe" in Bloomington, Indiana, was one such living child starved to death in a modern hospital. We ask again, What is man?

• Traditional language and expectations in male-female relationships are under constant assault. The more radical expressions of feminism have led to stronger reactions, especially in conservative religious circles. People on all sides of this debate are questioning the meaning of their humanity.

• The blatant and overt homosexuality in American culture is matched by extreme reactions of those described as suffering from homophobia. In the meantime, some (presumably) evangelical writers now advise capitulation to the unchangeable fact of homosexuality in our society. How do these issues relate to man as male and female?

• The issues of euthanasia and compassionate suicide pacts raise in new ways the meaning of life; quality of life becomes the new catch-phrase of our day. At what point is it no longer important to be man?

• Pornography, violence against the person, racial and social strife, child abuse and molestation, constant attention to arms and militarism—such are the stresses of our day. William Golding's morality story *Lord of the Flies* spoke of bestial behavior among children. Such behavior is found in our own day among adults. A young woman in a North End bar in New Bedford, Massachusetts, was recently the victim of a two-hour gang rape, during which onlookers encircled the victim and her attackers and screamed, "Go for it!" What is man?

• Computer technology is now so advanced that once erstwhile dreams of A.I. (artificial intelligence) seem nearly within reach. Computers are becoming "more human," and people less so. What is man . . . and what is machine?

• Then, with the terrors of our nuclear age, there are those who suspect the entire question is moot in any event. For if man is about to destroy himself, does it really matter who or what he is?

• And thoughts of God? They are now androgynous. God the Father is now called the Mother/Father; Christ is not Son but Child. Only the Holy Spirit is immune from change, and only because in English this term is not viewed to be sexist. What is man when we do not even know what to call God?

What is man? What is man in such a world?

Many who have a commitment to biblical faith are rightly disturbed about these new issues. Many Christian people lay the principal blame for these new realities at the door of secular humanists. As a matter of fact, there are many secular humanist philosophers who are equally as disturbed about some of these issues as those Christians who speak against the new scapegoat.

It is a fitting improbability that the answer to the question concerning the nature of man is to be found in the very text in which the question was first asked. David's question, "What is man?" is answered in his own Psalm. And the answer is surprising. For the biblical viewpoint turns out to be *humanism*—not humanism of the secular stripe, but theistic humanism—*humanism in praise of God*.

As we explore in this book the dimensions of the eighth Psalm, you and I will learn to reaffirm the biblical dignity of man in this age of dreadful assault upon humanity.

In this book, you and I, by God's mercy, will come to grips with the wonder of being human. We will learn to answer the question What is man? by the strong affirmative, Man is majestic! As male and female, man reflects the wonder of the Creator whose image man bears. As male and female in Christ, you and I may recover the fullness of God's intention in majesty and may live lives to his glory in these darkest of days.

We will learn to be true humanists, for humanism, rightly defined in Christ, is our divinely intended glory.

May Jesus the Man encourage us to be truly human!

PART 1

THE MYSTERY OF MAN

What is man that you are mindful of him,
the son of man that you care for him?
King David

Yet man is born to trouble
as surely as sparks fly upward.
Eliphaz the Temanite

What does man gain from all his labor
at which he toils under the sun?
Qohelet of Jerusalem

Chapter 1

Whither Man?

Where is man going in our brave new world? As we approach the twilight years of the second millennium A.D., all of us must consider again basic issues of identity and direction. We wonder with renewed concern where the age is taking us. We ask with growing apprehension, where do we fit in the scheme of things? More fundamentally, we renew an ancient question: What does it mean to be man?

Almost Human

"Now watch this," he said.

He hardly needed to encourage us. We were already nearly mesmerized by his demonstration of a sophisticated new minicomputer. For most of us, this was the first hands-on experience we had ever had with such a machine.

The ebullient demonstrator then reached out and touched the CRT screen with his index finger. Instantly the information on the screen was reconfigured. We all gasped.

"Did you see that?" he asked. "When I touched the screen, the computer responded. It responded to my touch! It's almost human!"

"Almost human"—what is that?

Just a few months after this experience, *Time* magazine broke a fifty-five year tradition. For over half a century, this newsmagazine has made news itself by choosing the Man of the Year in its January issue. But the Man of the Year in January 1983 was no man—it was a machine. The index blurb to the cover story explained: "Since no one person dominated this process, *Time's* Man of the Year for 1982 is not a man but the computer itself."

The double-page cover pictured plaster people sitting passively before active computers. The cover story itself was not without irony. Writer Frederic Golden's computer inexplicably swallowed his initial story on the new computer generation. Another malfunction was reported to writer Jay Cocks: "They told me that his computer was down. I envisioned an old hippie having a fit of depression."

But finally the story was written under the bold heading: "A New World Dawns."

And in such a world, what does it mean to be almost human? More important, what does it mean to be truly human?

A New World

We are in a new world and not just because of the computer. For those of us who live in North America, that new world has come with stunning rapidity. As in the case of children at Disneyland we have hardly had time to catch our breath before we are on a new adventure. But unlike Disneyland, not all of the adventures are pleasant. Many of us find these new adventures difficult to accept. The new world has us reeling.

Think of the changes in our new world in the mores expressed in the popular arts. Can it be that less than twenty-five years ago, Allen Drury's daring novel *Advise and Consent* turned on the dilemma of a public figure being exposed as a homosexual? Such a plot line would hardly cause a ripple today.

The word "homosexual" has been changed to "gay." The closet doors are open. What formerly was a matter of private shame has become an issue of perverse and public pride. Associations of terms that our parents would never have dreamed of making are uttered today with abandon. A few months ago, on the campus of an evangelical theological seminary, I found myself a participant in a public forum of "Christian Gay Activists." Passages of the Bible that we have traditionally understood to be condemnations of homosexual acts were interpreted by the panelists to be condemnations of bigotry of the non-homosexual Christian. In the newspaper of that city a Protestant bishop, while assuring his readers that he is "straight," spoke of a dream that he has of the day when the church will openly sanction marriages of homosexual partners. In the Newspeak of our new world, perversion is a term that seems to be used only of those who hesitate in sharing such dreams. It is the traditionalist who has become perverse.

Can anyone who has seen current situation comedy on television believe that such programs could have come within three decades of "Ozzie and Harriet" or "I Love Lucy"? It is a new world. It is an uncomfortable world for those who cherish fidelity and constancy in marriage (between a man and a woman!). In this new world the values of traditional biblical morality are the new endangered species.

Can the reader of *People* magazine really be aware that it was not too many years ago when an exceedingly gifted and popular screen actress left the United States in shame because of the scandal of her private life? Such peccadillos of media personalities are so routine today as to be merely the subjects of gossip for trivia buffs.

Is it really possible that it was only in 1973 that the U.S. Supreme Court presented its decision in *Roe v. Wade* that made abortion on demand as common as it is today in the United States?

Our age is new. It is frighteningly new. In our new age we ask again, Whither man?

Hi-Tech and Old Values

The most demanding issues of our age appear to be the parallel rise of high technology and the demise of old values, and our corresponding sense of a loss of control.

The extraordinary technical advances of our time are accompanied by an extreme and debilitating moral permissiveness which promises in time to break down even the values and system that made both the advances and the permissiveness possible.[1]

This feeling of a loss of control in an age of high technology and moral degeneration is developed by Christian theologian Joseph Bayly in his stunning novel, *Winterflight*. In this novel, set in America in the not-too-distant future, the twin concepts of the rise of technology and the loss of old values present a world more frightening than Orwell's *1984*. One of the characters in Bayly's book, Dr. Price Berkowitz, explains the forces that led to the loss of control.

"It seems to me that a certain point of no return was passed in the early seventies, when the Supreme Court made abortion legal for any cause or none. I'm not blaming the Court—things had been heading up that way anyway. Then when people got accustomed to aborting a fetus, even a viable one, the medical researchers said, 'Look, why do we have to kill those babies? Why not use them for experiments?' At first there was an outcry, people—including some physicians—said it was immoral. But then pragmatism won the battle, as it always does. If a fetus can be torn to pieces, why can't an aborted fetus, a viable one, be kept alive and used in experiments, the same as rats and dogs and little pigs?"

"You make it sound so natural," Grace said.

"That's the way it seemed at the time. After that, it was just another logical step to destroy newborn infants, normally born ones that were found to have congenital problems. Why should parents or the government spend money on their care? It was maybe five years later that someone had the great idea of the organ factory."[2]

The organ factory is used for the unwanted persons of the brave new world. The upper portions of their brains are killed. But they are kept alive and growing so that they may be used to donate spare parts for the beautiful people. Dr. Berkowitz exclaims:

> "Can't you see it? This whole country's cursed. Jews and Wasps, Blacks, Chicanos, everybody. It's cursed with health and intelligence and beauty. Everyone's so damned beautiful, so damned bright, so damned healthy."[3]

Perfect health is a blessing when it is provided by God. Perfect health will be a particular blessing of the coming kingdom of his Christ. But perfect health brought about by the machinations of evil men is a terrible curse. Beauty, intelligence, and health that are achieved by genetic manipulation and by the destruction or removal of all that is ugly, feeble, and sick is no blessing at all.

Loss of Control

The most terrible issue of our day is the public fear that on some day in some way modern technology will run amuck and will bring about the end of civilization, perhaps even the end of the human species.

The renowned German theologian Helmut Thielicke speaks of the high anxiety that this line of thought produces:

> The tension between our ability to plan all things, to achieve infinite technological extension, and our simultaneous inability to master our being in the world, our human existence, causes great anxiety. This anxiety finds expression in the question: Where is it all leading? It arises out of the unforeseeability of technological possibilities, but even more so out of an obscure and mostly unconsidered awareness that the gap between technology and human control might become even greater.[4]

Whatever our orientation might be, we face anew in our age the question of the nature and destiny of man. What hope is there for man in the era of his discontent? Thielicke says that the present level of anxiety demands that we think. "What we think about are the questions of our final Whence and Whither, which were long since thought to be dead, buried in the passion to master the world."[5]

This book is intended to help you, the reader, ask again the basic questions of your existence: What is man and where is he going?

Chapter 1, Notes

1. James Montgomery Boice, *The Sovereign God*, vol. 1 of *Foundations of the Christian Faith* (Downers Grove, Ill.: InterVarsity Press, 1978), 17.

2. Joseph Bayly, *Winterflight* (Waco, Tex.: Word Books, 1981), 38-39.

3. Ibid., 39.

4. Helmut Thielicke, *Being Human . . . Becoming Human: An Essay in Christian Anthropology*, trans. Geoffrey W. Bromiley (Garden City, N.Y.: Doubleday, 1984), 295.

5. Ibid.

To lose one's faith—surpass
The loss of an Estate—
Because Estates can be
Replenished—faith cannot—

Inherited with Life—
Belief—but once—can be—
Annihilate a single clause—
And Being's—Beggary—
—Emily Dickinson (c. 1862)

Chapter 2

The Shift to Secularism

"**Y**ou've come a long way, baby."

These words speak of more than the newly gained "right" of women to join men in using substances that are likely to be harmful to their bodies. These words are also indicative of the processes of change that are so active in our modern culture.

One does not have to be prescient to observe that our culture is undergoing significant change. The aspect of change that is particularly troubling to the man or woman of faith in our day is the headlong rush to secularism. A few decades ago the words "under God" were included in the pledge of allegiance to the American flag. Earlier the legend "in God we trust" was added to our coinage. Such statements of national public sentiment would not likely be forwarded today. We wonder, in fact, how long they will survive. More indicative slogans of current popular culture are likely to be "Grab the gusto."

That is, when one moves from the person of God
    as the center of life,
        the basis of meaning,
            the reason for existence;
    then "Being's—Beggary—."

Christ as the Center of Education

The acceleration of secularism in our age is so prominent that it is difficult to ignore. Nevertheless, a bit of a review of the situation will heighten our appreciation of the current crisis.

The change in orientation in American culture from the colonial period to our own day is so dramatic that it is difficult to believe in retrospect. Education in the early colonies was oriented toward the glory of God. Education was primarily for the preparation of the Christian ministry. Those educated in other disciplines still had their center on the person of Christ. The mottos of wisdom in Scripture were taken seriously: There is no true wisdom apart from the fear of Yahweh; Christ is the center and focus of all wisdom.

Consider, for example, the statement given by the trustees of Harvard College shortly after its founding in 1636:

> Let every student be plainly instructed, and earnestly pressed to consider well [that the] main end of his life and studies is to know God and Jesus Christ . . . and therefore to lay Christ in the bottom, as the only foundation of all sound knowledge and learning.[1]

Modern students at Harvard and other universities in North America—indeed in all lands—would do well to seize these words as their basis in higher education. It would also be nice if goat meat were more tender or that the dodo bird were to be rediscovered in Mauritius.

Hebrew and Culture

"You've come a long way, baby."

How far have we come? One example comes from the decline of the discipline of the study of Hebrew language. A working knowledge of Hebrew, along with Greek, was once regarded as essential to civilization and culture in the West because of the priority of studying the biblical text. Among the earliest chairs of learning in major universities in the West was the chair of Hebrew language.

But things have changed. "We have gone a long way since Ezra Stiles, president of Yale University, himself taught the freshmen and other classes Hebrew, and in 1781 delivered his commencement address in Hebrew."[2] A long way indeed! Today, even in the most conservative Protestant theological seminaries, backward-looking purists have to fight the waves of relevant practicality to maintain even a small place for Hebrew studies in the curriculum. In one seminary's recent survey of alumni to assess curricular needs, the study of Hebrew was regarded as slightly less important than course work on the use of office equipment.

It is important to note that the roots for President Stiles's enthusiasm for Hebraic studies lay not only in his interest in and love for the Scripture, but was the legacy of early European humanism. While it is not generally known among Christians today, the modern study of Hebrew language by non-Jewish scholars is a consequence of the early Renaissance beginning in the second half of the fifteenth century.

In 1516/17 the texts of the Hebrew and Greek Testaments were published in Venice and Basel. Luther's role in the Reformation was affected considerably by his access to the original languages of the Bible in these newly published texts. His own great accomplishment in the translation of the Scriptures not only formed the solid base for the Reformation, but it also established the modern shape of the German language.

By 1600, "practically all of Hebraic literature—biblical, rabbinic, medieval—was available to Christian Hebraists, and many scholars who specialized in other areas of Humanist interest had at least a fair working knowledge of what were by then regarded as standard Jewish writings."[3]

Today we have better biblical texts and linguistic tools for their study than ever in postbiblical history. But with all the tools available, there is little enthusiasm to use them. Departments of Religious Studies are no longer the centers of the great universities of the West. Theology, once the Queen of Sciences, is now like Cinderella after midnight, her clothes again in tatters. Who knows if any one cares to look for her slipper.

The Growing Up of Civilization

Our movement from a model of culture that is at least ostensibly centered in the person of God is viewed by many as a part of the growing up process of civilization. As a primitive savage in a benighted land moves from superstition to science, so culture in the West has moved from a center in God and the study of his works to a brave new world in which God is neither desired nor needed.

The movement to our present age of secularism did not come all at once or with unanimity. But certain forces were prominent in bringing about the new view of man that exists in our modern world. Among these were the influences of the work and writings of Copernicus, Darwin, and Freud. As Thielicke points out, it was Freud who spoke of "three great humblings" that have led to the modern relativizing of humanity.

> Copernicus was responsible for the first when he showed that the earth and humanity are not the center of the universe. He forced upon us the startling insight that we are an insignificant marginal phenomenon, mere dust set on a particle of dust. Darwin brought the second humbling when with his theory of evolution he demonstrated our animal ancestry. This seemed to demand the conclusion that we are no longer privileged as compared with the animal kingdom, that we no longer enjoy the prerogative of divine likeness, but that we have to regard ourselves as higher animals. The third humbling was effected by Freud himself. For he had made it plain to us that from the root up we are not under the control of the self and its will but of a complex of subconscious impulses.[4]

The effects of these three humblings in changing the thought of modern man are incalculable. We have grown up in a different age than our forefathers. In the new world, God is no longer at the center. Man has to find his own way. For some people that will lead to absurdity, for others to despair, for some to making a mark for good out of well-meaning altruism, and for many to grab what gusto there is, "for you only go around once."

Religion in the New World

For religion to have any role in the new world, many believe it must come to terms with the three humblings of Copernicus, Darwin, and Freud. Hence the process of secularization has also been active in theology in the last century. Again we mention three names—Wellhausen, Schweitzer, and Bultmann—who have contributed to this secularization.

Old Testament studies in the last century have been dominated by an approach associated particularly with the name Julius Wellhausen (1844-1918). His *Prolegomena to the History of Ancient Israel* was published a little over a century ago. Wellhausen was not the originator of the viewpoint he espoused, but was the one who did the most to popularize the theory that has come to be known as "higher criticism" of the Bible. His influence and importance in the development of this theory are difficult to exaggerate. Wellhausen's position in the critical study of the Old Testament is "somewhat analogous to that of Darwin in the intellectual history of modern times."[5]

The importance of the work of Wellhausen was not only in assigning various strata of the Pentateuch to differing sources (the now familiar putative sources J, E, D, P), but in his presentation of the unified theory of biblical origins that was essentially secular in nature. Supernaturalism, miracles, divine intervention, inspiration—these and other marks of the inner witness of Scripture to its divine origin were dismissed. Israel was presented by Wellhausen as a people with a marked gift for religion, as the Greeks were noted for culture and the Romans for order. Essentially, his presentation is the application of evolution to the religious ideals of the Bible. What results is a Bible for nonbelievers.[6] At least one scholar has gone so far as to assert that Wellhausen "made forever impossible the belief on the part of the intelligent portion of humanity that the Old Testament writings were a supernatural communication of the Holy

Spirit."[7] It seems that modesty is not highly prized by certain members of the scholarly community.

Jesus, Faith, and History

New Testament and theological studies followed suit with the new secularization of the Christian religion. Albert Schweitzer (1875-1965) was an illustrious figure of modern times. In recognition of his work as a selfless and giving humanitarian, he was awarded the Nobel peace prize in 1952. In some ways Schweitzer was the true Renaissance man: philosopher, theologian, scholar, musician, physician, missionary.

One aspect of the career of Schweitzer that is perhaps not as well known as his work as a jungle medical doctor in Lambaréné (in present-day Gabon) was his scholarly study of the Gospels to ascertain the historicity of the life of Jesus of Nazareth. In his *Quest of the Historical Jesus* (first published in 1906), Schweitzer came to a decidedly negative conclusion.

> The Jesus of Nazareth who came forward publicly as the Messiah, who preached the ethic of the Kingdom of God, who founded the Kingdom of heaven upon earth, and died to give His work its final consecration, never had any existence. He is a figure designed by rationalism, endowed with life by liberalism, and clothed by modern theology in an historical garb.[8]

Where Copernicus had led to the conclusion that the earth was no longer the center of the universe, Schweitzer was denying the historical credibility of the life of the Savior Jesus.

Close upon the heels of this secularization of the Gospels came the radical demythologizing approach of Rudolf Bultmann (1884-1976) to the New Testament and Christian theology. Essentially, Bultmann's approach was that of the secularist, as we can see from this summary by George Eldon Ladd.

> The modern man had learned through astronomy and geology that there is no heaven up in the skies and no hell down in the earth. Bacteriology has taught him

that sickness is due to microbes and germs, not to demons or evil spirits. The biblical picture of a "three-decker universe," i.e., of heaven above, hell below, and earth between, with its descent of God's Son from heaven to earth, His return to heaven after His resurrection, and His coming again from heaven—this cannot be the gospel. Such ideas have no relevance in the twentieth century but must be understood as an elaborate first-century myth which the modern man can no longer accept because it is diametrically opposed to the nature of the world and history as the scientific era has established it.[9]

For these reasons, Bultmann sought to reinterpret the basic ideas of the gospel in terms that would be acceptable to twentieth-century man. The ancient myths were of no meaning to moderns. The reader should not cut out these myths from the Bible (as the older liberal approach suggested), but the reader should reinterpret them into modern meanings. This is what he termed "demythologizing."

In Bultmann's view the real Jesus of history can never be known. But it is not important that he should be known, except as the modern reader responds to him in an existential moment.

We do not wish to imply that the lines of thought of Wellhausen, Schweitzer, and Bultmann have gone unchallenged. Both liberal and orthodox writers have sought to challenge or to redirect these points of view. But there has been considerable fallout from these secular religionists in popular culture. The secularism of our age is not alone the result of the upheavals brought about by Copernicus, Darwin, and Freud.

The Rose in the Desert

An illustration of the secularizing process may be seen in the humble postage stamp. The expression "the wilderness will blossom like the rose" is a familiar aspect of the biblical prophecy of the coming reign of King Jesus. These words of Isaiah 35:1 (where the NIV has the more accurate but unexpected "crocus" for "rose") have to do with more than just a garden in an unusual location. The prophecy concerns the delight of all of creation at the establishment of God's rule on earth. Read the words slowly to sense their beauty and thrust:

> The desert and the parched land will be glad;
>   the wilderness will rejoice and blossom.
> Like the crocus, it will burst into bloom;
>   it will rejoice greatly and shout for joy.
> The glory of Lebanon will be given to it,
>   the splendor of Carmel and Sharon;
> they will see the glory of the LORD,
>   the splendor of our God.
>
> (Isaiah 35:1-2)

When the modern state of Israel completed the great task of building the national water carrier in the early fifties, the department of posts issued stamps to commemorate the event. One of the stamps[10] depicts a brilliant rose growing in the starkness of the Negev. The stem of the rose is a stylized water pipe, and that which supports the pipe is the hand of man rising out of the earth. That is, the expectations of the messianic age are being realized by the state. Since God has not brought the wilderness into bloom, man will do it for him.

Life in a Secular Age

How does one live in such an age when faith in the God of Scripture is lost and man is the measure of things? Some live in a never-ending pursuit of happiness. Thomas Jefferson, in the Declaration of Independence, spoke of the "pursuit of Happiness" as an unalienable right. In a contemporary women's magazine, known for its espousal of a secular viewpoint, one writer says, "Now, more than two hundred years later, ours is still one of but a few countries where the pursuit of happiness is not only held self-evident by the government, it is almost required. Indeed, it may be our greatest economic and political resource. It is certainly our national passion."[11]

One way to live in the secular age is to adopt the motto of a certain type of advertising. Let's go for the gusto, and go for it as long as we can. As George Burns argues, the way to make it to the age of 100 or more "is to be sure you make it to 99"; for, he suggests, "with a good positive attitude and a little bit of luck, there's no reason you can't live to be 100. Once you've done that you've really got it made, because very few people die over 100."[12]

The concept of the Scripture, "Just as man is destined to die once, and after that to face judgment" (Hebrews 9:27), seems hardly relevant to many in modern culture. Admittedly there are those who eschew hedonism and egoism and who live lives that contribute significantly to society. Not all have chosen the route of self-gratification in our day. Nonetheless, even for one who is selfless and giving, a life apart from God is ultimately a life that is not worth living.

> When Man is the measure of all things,
>   there is no need for God;
> With the loss of faith, Being is beggared;
>   there is really no meaning for man—
>   Hence, grab, get, and glut!
> Eat, drink, and be merry!
> For you only go around once.

Chapter 2, Notes

1. Cited by James Montgomery Boice, *The Sovereign God*, vol. 1 of *Foundations of the Christian Faith* (Downers Grove, Ill.: InterVarsity Press, 1978), 9.

2. Harry M. Orlinsky, "The Textual Criticism of the Old Testament," in *The Bible and the Ancient Near East*, ed. G. Ernest Wright (Garden City, N.Y.: Doubleday, 1965), 141. An account of the career of Stiles at Yale is given by Roland H. Bainton, *Yale and the Ministry* (New York: Harper, 1957), 69-72.

3. M. H. Goshen-Gottstein, "Humanism and the Rise of Hebraic Studies: From Christian to Jewish Renaissance," in *The Word of the Lord Shall Go Forth: Essays in Honor of David Noel Freedman*, ed. Carol L. Meyers and M. O'Connor (Winona Lake, Ind.: Eisenbrauns, 1983), 693.

4. Helmut Thielicke, *Being Human . . . Becoming Human: An Essay in Christian Anthropology*, trans. Geoffrey W. Bromiley (Garden City, N.Y.: Doubleday & Co., 1984), 29.

5. Herbert F. Hahn with Horace D. Hummel, *The Old Testament in Modern Research* (Philadelphia: Fortress Press, 1966), 11.

6. First published in German in 1878, Wellhausen's work is still available in English: *Prolegomena to the History of Ancient Israel,* preface by W. Robertson Smith (Cleveland: The World Publishing Co., 1957). One of the finest critiques of Wellhausen's work is that given by Herman Wouk in *This Is My God* (New York: Doubleday & Co., 1959), 312-20.

7. Emil G. Kraeling, *The Old Testament Since the Reformation* (New York: Schocken Books, 1969), 95.

8. Albert Schweitzer, *Quest of the Historical Jesus,* trans. W. Montgomery (New York: Macmillan, 1948), 396, cited by Nils Alstrup Dahl, "The Problem of the Historical Jesus," in *Kerygma and History: A Symposium on the Theology of Rudolf Bultmann,* ed. Carl E. Braaten and Roy A. Harrisville (New York: Abingdon Press, 1962), 144.

9. George Eldon Ladd, *Rudolf Bultmann* (Chicago: InterVarsity Press, 1964), 20-21. The first book to read by Bultmann himself is *Jesus Christ and Mythology* (New York: Charles Scribner's Sons, 1958).

10. Minkus 121, 22 September 1953.

11. Leslie Glass, "What Is This Thing Called Happiness?" *Cosmopolitan,* (January 1984), 173.

12. George Burns, *How to Live to Be 100—Or More: The Ultimate Diet, Sex and Exercise Book* (New York: G. P. Putnam's Sons, 1983), 20, 177.

Lowborn men are but a breath,
the highborn are but a lie;
if weighed on a balance, they are nothing;
together they are only a breath.
King David

"Do not be afraid, O worm Jacob,
O little Israel,
for I myself will help you," declares the LORD,
your Redeemer, the Holy One of Israel.
The Prophet Isaiah

I was a groveling creature once,
And basely cleaved to earth;
I wanted spirit to renounce
The clod that gave me birth.

But God has breathed upon a worm,
And sent me from above
Wings such as clothe an angel's form,
The wings of joy and love.
—William Cowper (1779)

Chapter 3

A Breath, a Worm, a Man

*T*he principal question of our troubled age centers on the issue of what it really means to be human. "What is man?" is not merely a nifty examination question for the first year college course in philosophy. It is the burning issue of our day. The very survival of the species may hinge on our answer. While people everywhere are searching out the dimensions of this question, it is an issue of particular importance for the Christian. As we shall see, there is a sense in which all of theology will be affected by the answer we give.

A Breath, an Absurdity

When we turn to the text of Scripture to answer what it means to be human, we may well find that the Bible seems to point in a particularly negative direction. If one were to turn to Psalm 62:9, for example, one might come to a dark and dismal understanding of humanity:

> Lowborn men are but a breath,
>   the highborn are but a lie;
> if weighed on a balance, they are nothing;
>   together they are only a breath.

This verse, when read by itself and shorn of context, may lead one to an absurdist view of mankind that approximates that of the noted French author Albert Camus (1913-1960). If man is but a breath, whether of low station or high, then the human being is of no lasting value. There may be a temporary and relative value in being human, as Dr. Rieux, Camus's narrator, concludes at the end of his account of *The Plague*. Rieux's chronicle was written to present a memorial of injustice, "and to state quite simply what we learn in a time of pestilence: that there are more things to admire in men than to despise."[1] But this is of little pleasure to Rieux, for the joy of freed people is always in peril—new rats and new plagues are always ready to bring death in a happy city. Camus's brooding over the seeming meaninglessness of human existence led him to state, "Man is not entirely to blame, it was not he who started history; nor is he entirely innocent since he continues it."[2]

But Breath without God

Camus came to his unhappy conclusion about human existence in part because of his belief in a world devoid of the comfort that comes in believing in God or in absolute standards. Without God, man is but a breath. Without ultimate reality in him, life is absurd.

If we look again at the troubling words of Psalm 62:9, this time setting them in their context, we discover that these words really have nothing at all to do with the meaning and nature of being human. They refer rather to the true absurdity—a man living his life apart from God. The preceding verse speaks of the high meaning found in placing one's trust in Yahweh:

Trust in him at all times, O people;
 pour out your hearts to him,
 for God is our refuge.

The disparaging words about man as "but a breath" (v. 9) are set in the context of a man choosing to trust in God as the ultimate reality of life. One who decides instead to choose man as the object of trust is choosing a being whose existence is conditioned on his next breath. How silly to choose that which so easily perishes, when one might choose to trust in God, a "mighty rock" (v. 7), who endures forever!

Hence the issue in Psalm 62:9 is not the value and meaning of being man, but the folly of one living his life apart from strong confidence in God. By missing the links between these verses, one might make a critical error concerning who man is. Unfortunately, some Christian people miss such links far too often.

The Missing Links

For all their insistence upon the problem of "missing links" in the putative evolutionary models, some Christians display that a few of their own links are missing—the links of logic and continuity, the link of balance, and at times even the link of charity. Some of these links are missing because these Christian people have developed a subbiblical view of man.

A Spirit of Action and Reaction

In the first chapter of this book we noted some of the unpleasant changes in public morality and standards of behavior that have come upon us with a vengeance in the last couple of decades. Not only is there a depersonalizing of man in our hi-tech culture, there is a corresponding debasing of man in our permissive society. Traditional concepts of the family, of marriage, of human sexuality, and of public decency have changed so thoroughly in popular culture that we find ourselves in a new (and largely unpleasant) world.

The principal culprit in the unpleasantness of our culture is usually identified as "secular humanism," that approach to life in which God is ignored and man is magnified. Many books on the dangers of humanism occupy shelf space in Christian bookstores. Some of these books have had an immense readership and influence.

Moreover, people are beginning to act. They are no longer content to sit back and watch the slide of traditional values into the cultural malaise of our day. All of a sudden we find ourselves inundated with mailings from active and aggressive organizations that are so numerous we have difficulty keeping them straight.

There are Christian coalitions for better television, for example, that have developed some clout in their threat to boycott sponsors and networks who present objectionable programming. There are coalitions of Christians against nearly every evil practice (or perceived wickedness) of our immoderately wicked age: Believers are fighting against pornography, against abortion, against euthanasia, against the nuclear freeze, against women's movements (ERA), against homosexuality, against state regulation of private schools, against atheistic evolution . . . and the list goes on.

Many of these action groups are to be applauded, joined, and supported. People who feel strongly about these issues should work on behalf of their goals. But the Christian should enter such action groups only after careful thought and reflection. "Extremism in the pursuit of liberty" is likely to fare as poorly in this decade as it did in the sixties.

It is especially in the environment of threat and hostility that one is likely to lose balance. I have certainly found this to be true in my own life. On occasions I have been defensive in my stance toward a certain position, and I have said things that surprised me because of the stridency and militancy of my words. Not long ago, when listening to a representative of a current moral position that I believe to be particularly distasteful, I said things that would have been better thought than expressed aloud. I charged the atmosphere and hurt the discussion.

There are many Christians today who seem to be reacting in similar fashion to the pressures of contemporary culture. The perceived rise of secular humanism has caused many to react strongly. Some of this response is undoubtedly understandable, even necessary. People who fail to react at all to hostile pressures will share the blame for the evils that may come in our age. But not all of the reactions have been based on fact or presented in balance.

There are several areas of acute concern in the evangelical

community today—areas in which the nature of man plays an especially important role.

Abortion

Abortion on demand as the "right" of a woman over the use of the tissues of her own body is rightly judged by the Christian as an exceedingly evil perversion in our culture. I myself have spoken on the steps of the state capitol in Oregon in a rally against the decision of the Supreme Court to permit abortion on demand. I yield to none in my abhorrence of this evil.[3]

Yet, even in this area of unquestionable evil, the Christian should learn to judge issues carefully. It is one thing to agree with the assessment that the current practice of abortion on demand is an unbiblical position. It is quite another to assert that abortion is always wrong in every circumstance. In our revulsion against the abuse of morality in taking away any rights of the unborn child, we may be guilty of acting and arguing in such a harsh manner that we do in fact deny the pregnant woman rights she genuinely has. In the case of a tubal pregnancy, for example, the developing fetus presents a case of material aggression against the life of the mother. Simply to say that abortion is wrong in all cases is not to meet the very real needs of that woman whose own life might be in jeopardy.

Evolution

The Apostle's Creed begins with the words, "I believe in God the Father Almighty, Maker of heaven and earth." This is the principal postulate of all Christian theology. Some people might imagine that the difficulty of a Christian reconciliation with the modern secular world view can be resolved simply by having one skip past the first few chapters of the Bible. Actually, the doctrine of divine creation of the universe and all that is in it is so essential to the Christian faith that to deny creation is implicitly to deny the faith.

Creation then is not a minor issue. Christians should be expected to react strongly against the atheistic theories of origins that flood the media and fill the marketplace of ideas. Christians are especially likely to be disturbed when their children are presented nontheistic evolutionary theories of origins as fact, with only belittling or degrading references made to the dissent of faith. Christians cannot be expected to ignore what is essentially an assault on their faith. Further, a young Christian student is rarely a match for the teacher of the class when opportunity is given to challenge the assault.

Nonetheless, many feel that in recent days there have been errors in judgment by well-meaning believers that have done considerable harm for the presentation of a creationist position in public education. One such error is the argument (a specious one in my judgment) that creationism can be presented in the classroom in a scientific manner without religious overtones. "Scientific creationism" is in some ways an oxymoron. The "science" in this presentation is sometimes a nit-picking against a dominant theory rather than a fully developed induction of data. The "creationism" in this view is faulty, for how may one discuss creation without giving full attention to the Creator? It is simply disingenuous to argue that creation is not a religious issue.

A second error is the presentation of one model of creation as the alternative to all models of evolution. Certainly we cannot expect the proponents of evolution to maintain a static posture in their theories. But only one notion of creation was presented by the creationists in the recent debates and court trials, a position of a young earth created by God in one week of twenty-four-hour days. Furthermore, the impression was given that this viewpoint was the only possibility for those who hold to a high view of the Scriptures.

As a matter of fact, there are many evangelical scholars with the highest view of Scripture who are not at all comfortable with the "creation-science" model. One leading scholar, Dr. Walter L. Bradley, professor of mechanical engineering at Texas A & M, has given a compelling presentation of a model of creation different than the one before the general public. In his view, which he terms "progressive creationism," Bradley argues that the creation texts in Genesis may be interpreted as speaking of God working through both miracle and process.[4]

It may well be that Bradley's position will itself come under subsequent criticism by biblically informed scientific researchers. Other models may be presented in time that will be superior to this one. We dare not be premature in settling the issue of the Bible and science. We should not be willing to repeat the error of the church in the day of Galileo by putting all our credibility in one interpretive basket.

> To the Church, Galileo's new science was heresy; he was placed under house arrest until his death in 1641. Galileo was soon exonerated by his scientific community whose subsequent experiments gave additional proof of the heliocentricity of our solar system. Public acceptance of Galileo's finding was soon to follow. However, the Church did not formally exonerate Galileo until the spring of 1983, about 370 years after his discovery. The Church's error in theological interpretation was eventually corrected with increasing knowledge from natural revelation. Both science and theology would have benefited by a more rapid resolution of that disagreement.[5]

We have much to learn from such rash behavior. We dare not react merely out of anger or fear.

Government

Negative attitudes toward government is another area of considerable ferment in Christian circles in the United States. Increasingly, Christian leaders of the right are speaking of the government as a malevolent force that is out to destroy faith, church, and home. Conspiracy theories seem to be proliferating as in the 1950s. In the last few years numerous letters have been sent by well-meaning people to governmental agencies to protest contemplated actions. After a barrage of mail, word finally trickles back to the writers that the incident in question was entirely a mistake, based on an unfounded rumor.

Other campaigns of protest are based on misinformation or

specific bias. A current letter on my desk was written to encourage me to send the following form message to the president of the United States:

> I am outraged over governmental harassment of churches and private schools, and I'm calling on you to help bring the IRS and other federal agencies into line.
>
> The Constitution guarantees all Americans absolute religious freedom and government agencies are willfully trampling this constitutional right.

In fact, the Constitution does not give an absolute guarantee of religious freedom at all, as polygamous Mormons and drug-cult religionists will readily attest. And what is the specific issue that calls for "outrage" and speaks of "governmental harassment" of Christian faith? A small church-related school in a midwestern state refuses to hire accredited teachers to teach their students. One teacher who had accreditation and who was fully in sympathy with the school and its religious nature volunteered to teach for a time without pay in order to help the school meet state regulations. The pastor of the church would have none of it—that would be a violation of principle. Apparently it is preferable to have pastor and parents in jail as martyrs to an oppressive government than to have qualified teachers for one's children. One cannot help wondering if the same concern for principle applies in the selection of physicians to care for the physical needs of one's child. Are regulations for licensing of doctors unnecessary intrusions of the state?

Since we live in a world where some governments truly are oppressive against religious freedom, it appears to be a profligate use of our own freedom of worship and assembly to behave in such a manner. We seem not to have learned the danger of calling "Wolf!" prematurely. Further, the letter I cited above contains a measure of irony. The shrill call that government is out to destroy the church was released over the signature of a congressman, presumably a part of the very government he denounced.

Education

In some Christian circles the fear of humanism in public education has reached near panic levels. Attitudes are presented in some cases that are alarming in their naiveté. I recently conversed with the principal of a Christian school in a distant state who had decided to drop one well-known curriculum published by a fundamentalist institution. He told me even those materials were humanist in nature.

I was surprised since I knew the nature of the materials in question and I asked him what could be humanist about it. He answered that the program contained pagan stories such as "Hansel and Gretel." He said, "You know how much witchcraft and stuff is in that story. We don't want anything like that!"

I responded briefly concerning the role of imagination in little children, the place of the fairy tale in our heritage of literature, how the story of "Hansel and Gretel" is a morality story, and described the underlying theology in this account—a factor that is truly significant and moving. I reminded him of the wonderful opera by Humperdinck. In short, I gave him both barrels. It was all to no avail. No "humanism" was to be allowed!

Shortly thereafter I had a series of conversations with parents in the community who told me a number of horror stories about the public school. Acts of outright rebellion, threats against the life of a mother by her teen-age son, stories of children claiming Constitutional rights not to obey their parents—these were told with conviction (and enthusiasm).

"This is exactly what the schools are teaching," one parent said. "The schools are teaching children to rebel against their parents, to threaten them, to disobey them!"

"It's the counselors," another said. "They have told our children that any parental discipline is child abuse. This is why we need Christian schools!"

I was so disturbed by these reports and the vehemence with which they were related that I did something out of character for me. I went to the high school in that city and asked to speak with the head of the counseling department. Without saying anything about myself other than my name, I related these several allegations to the counselor and asked him to respond.

His response was one of amazement. He sat back, then leaned forward and said, "Don't these people realize that we are parents as well? Why would we desire to set children against their parents? And if we set children against their parents, what hope would we have for any discipline here in the school?" He then wondered why parents who had such strong concerns had never called to discuss them with him. It is often the case, he judged, that the very youngsters who have the most difficulty in school are the ones whose parents are the least cooperative.

I then commented on the decorative artwork on the wall behind him—a cross and a fish. I asked if these symbols had any special meaning for him. He smiled broadly and affirmed that they meant a great deal to him. He volunteered that he was an evangelical Christian, an active member of his church, and that he strove to relate his faith to his work as a counselor at the school.

It was my turn to respond with amazement. In a climate of fear and distrust, Christian parents were willing to believe nearly every negative thing they heard about their public school. By saying, "That's what they teach in the schools," these people were engaging in character assassination against a Christian brother.

I have no reason to believe that all is well with public education in the United States or elsewhere. Undoubtedly there are many subtle as well as overt assaults upon the Christian faith of students that transpire regularly in many schools. In some cases the only option for troubled parents and their children is to change to private schools. But those who promote Christian schools should speak truthfully about the benefits of their own programs and not falsely of the failures of public education. Further, Christian teachers who serve the community in public education should be encouraged in their work, and not be made to feel guilty of aiding the humanist conspiracy.

Life Style
    Another area of concern in our study of man is the issue of Christian life style. Some Christians tend at times to confuse is-

sues of genuine significance with matters of merely parochial importance. Genuinely dehumanizing practices such as abortion are lumped together with petty issues of Christian deportment and life style, such as the length of one's hair or the use of makeup. Attacks on the vile abuse of pornography sometimes extend to sweeping condemnations of genuine literary art whose subjects do not fit the tastes of the angry.

The Bible presents examples in both Testaments of people who confuse the splinter in another's eye with the log in their own. Both Jewish and Christian people have tended to err in majoring on the minors and missing the truly important.

(Speaking of the truly important: It has been related to me that my books will not be carried in the bookstores of certain Christian colleges because my picture on the covers shows me with a beard. It is a mercy that editions of the Bible do not carry pictures of Moses or other biblical writers.)

In one of his engaging detective novels, Jewish author Harry Kemelman describes a group of nine men gathered for the morning prayers at their synagogue. The prayer could not begin until the tenth man arrived. Kemelman takes us into the midst of the impatient men, each with prayer shawl and phylacteries in place—symbols of devotion to the Lord. We listen to their whispered conversations of plans for raw business deals, betrayals of wives and seductions, and other indecencies. These men are plotting evil while in the posture of prayer. What a confusion of letter and spirit.

Christians often make the same confusion. We know of Christian schools, for instance, where the fear of our permissive culture has caused them to enact excessive rules that belittle students and demean their very humanity. We understand the legitimate complaints of Christian parents about open student cohabitation in university dorm rooms. We agree that this is not "growing up"—it is an evil and a perversion of God's gift of sexuality that is weakening the fabric of our society.

But we do not aid the growing up of young people when we put such crimps in their life style that the following announcement was deemed necessary in the chapel period of one Christian college: "Students should observe that there is one legitimate exception to the rule concerning no physical contact of any kind between men and women students. If a male student happens to see a female student about to fall to the ground, it is permissible to touch her to break her fall. However, we shall not tolerate any young woman making a practice of falling." It seems that a young woman in a long dress fell on the bleachers in the school gym. Several fellows watched her fall and refused to help her up, lest they be reported for infringing the no-contact rule. Under the new dispensation these fellows might have helped her, but only on the first fall! Such attitudes belittle man.

Wherever there is law there is talmud. The pedestrian and picayune theological debates of some early rabbis and of some medieval monks seem to be matched point for petty point by the modern talmudists of the church.

It is still customary among strict hasidic Jewish men to avoid all sight and touch (and presumably thought) of women until the moment of their marriage. They are actually trained to think that women do not exist, at least not yet for them. Myrna Alexander, well known for her books on Bible studies for women, has told me of the time that she fell to the ground on a street in an orthodox section of Jerusalem. The young hasids paid her only the sufficient attention that allowed them not to step on her as they walked over her while she lay prostrate—and hurting—on the ground. Perhaps here are roots of the "no-touching" rules of some of our Christian colleges, at least for those "who make a practice of falling."

Morality

One further influence of humanism that concerns evangelicals is the general sphere of public morality. We have already touched on some of these issues. But it is worth noting that the moral issues regularly raised are few and of a similar type. Note, for example, the limited moral agenda emphasized in this letter from the Moral Majority:

Just look at what's happening here in America:

- Homosexual teachers have invaded the class-rooms, and the pulpits of our churches.
- Smut peddlers sell their pornographic books under the protection of the U.S. Constitution!
- And X-rated movies are allowed in almost every community because there is no legal definition of obscenity.
- Meanwhile, right in our own homes the television screen is full of R-rated movies and sex and violence.
- Believe it or not, we are the first civilized nation in history to legalize abortion—in the late months of pregnancy! Murder![6]

Homosexuality, smut, obscenity, R-rated movies, and abortion are unpleasant issues that do confront us—and we need to face them. But these are not the only moral demands of our age. One theological seminary, which states strongly its agreement with the pressing demands of these issues, adds some necessary addenda:

We want to do all we can to understand the causes of and to support basic solutions to human hunger in our world;

we intend to promote peace-making in the world and to press a call for limitation of arms—nuclear and others—by the nations;

we aim to combat in our own and other societies the inhumanity and injustice of racism—including anti-Semitism—sexism, and other discriminating ideologies;

we wish to enlarge our care about crime to include concern for the condition of our prisons,
the fairness of our judicial systems,
the effectiveness of our law enforcement,

and the compassion due victims of crime and
their families;

we plan to apply Christian principles of stewardship
to our society's policies for the protection of our environment

and to support the call for simpler life styles which
reflect care in the use of the earth's resources;

we desire to question a world economy which retards
the development of poorer countries by perpetuating
their dependence on richer ones.[7]

Perhaps no listing of moral issues will satisfy all evangelicals. But in my judgment the great advantage of the above statement is that it seeks to broaden our base of moral awareness in
the public sector. All of these items bear on genuine humanity.

Worm and Man

The current debate over secular humanism has reached a
fever pitch in some quarters. Some issues are raised to the panic
level, with overstatements and exaggeration that lead to pettiness and provincialism.

In some presentations, man is described in the basest of
terms with a loss of the biblical balance between the wickedness
of man and the dignity of being human. In some constructs of
the wickedness and unrighteousness of man—which no Christian dare deny—corresponding triumphs of humanity are mis-
judged, ignored, or debased. Biblical passages that affirm
man's inability to gain a righteous standing before God are used
to deny the wonders of what man is and can do. Soteriology is
confused with achievement. The issue of a relationship with
God is confused with issues of dignity and worth in being
human.

Man is to be viewed realistically by the Christian. Without
God, there is a sense in which we may say that man is nothing;
as a substitute for God, man is but a breath:

> Lowborn men are but a breath,
>   the highborn are but a lie;
> if weighed on a balance, they are nothing;
>   together they are only a breath.
>   (Psalm 62:9)

Apart from God there is a sense in which we may say that man is a worm; without the salvation of Yahweh, man is quite unable to help himself:

> "Do not be afraid, O worm Jacob,
>   O little Israel,
> for I myself will help you," declares
>   the LORD,
>   your Redeemer, the Holy One of Israel.
>   (Isaiah 41:14)

Only with the infusion of the breath of God may man the worm be metamorphosed into the winged creature who flies with joy and love to adorn the Creator with great praise:

> I was a groveling creature once,
>   And basely cleaved to earth;
> I wanted spirit to renounce
>   The clod that gave me birth.

> But God has breathed upon a worm,
>   And sent me from above
> Wings such as clothe an angel's form,
>   The wings of joy and love.
>   (William Cowper)

But there is more to man than breath or worm. In the next chapter we shall see that the proper response to secular humanism in our day is not a degrading of man, but a radical theistic humanism. In view of the Incarnation, the idea of man as a worm is a mockery. In fact, to be truly human is to be majestic. "Worminess" in man is a distortion, not the ideal of the Creator.

Chapter 3, Notes

1. Albert Camus, *The Plague,* trans. Stuart Gilbert, reprinted in *Nobel Prize Library: Albert Camus and Winston Churchill* (New York: Helvetica Press, 1971), 157.

2. Cited by Pierre de Boisdeferre, "The Life and Works of Albert Camus," ibid., 159. *The Plague [La Peste]* was published first in 1947. For his works, which also include *The Stranger [L'Étranger]* (1942), Camus was awarded the Nobel Prize for literature in 1957. The citation concluded with these words: "Beyond his [Camus's] incessant affirmation of the absurdity of the human condition is no sterile negativism. This view of things is supplemented in him by a powerful imperative, a 'nevertheless,' an appeal to the will which incites to revolt against absurdity and which, for that reason, creates a value" (p. 5).

3. I have written a booklet on the abortion issue in which I have attempted to state both my abhorrence of the evil act as well as my compassion for the woman facing the critical decision about her future. Ronald B. Allen, *Abortion: When Does Life Begin?* (Portland, Ore.: Multnomah Press, 1984).

4. Dr. Bradley's paper, "The Trustworthiness of Scripture in Areas Relating to Natural Science," was presented in November 1982 at the conference on hermeneutics held in Chicago and sponsored by the International Council on Biblical Inerrancy. The papers of this conference are published as *Hermeneutics, Inerrancy and the Bible: Papers from ICBI Summit II,* ed. Earl D. Radmacher and Robert D. Preus (Grand Rapids: Zondervan Publishing House, 1984).

5. This quotation is from a manuscript on the Bible and science being prepared for publication by Dr. Walter P. Dyke, a physicist, inventor, and naturalist of McMinnville, Oregon. Used by permission.

6. Letter of Jerry Falwell, cited by Robert E. Webber, *Secular Humanism: Threat and Challenge* (Grand Rapids: Zondervan Publishing House, 1982), 59.

7. Section IV-A from "Mission Beyond the Mission," a statement adopted by the trustees and faculty of Fuller Theological Seminary (Pasadena, Calif.: Fuller Theological Seminary, 25 September 1983). Used by permission.

I am a humanist. In truth, I believe it is only a thoroughgoing Christian who can ever have a right to that name.
J. I. Packer, *Knowing Man*

Chapter 4

Humanism— False and True

*M*ake no mistake about it. There is a potent force in the world today that has no place for God and no room for faith in his Christ. In this conception of reality, man believes himself to be his own definition of meaning, the maker of his own destiny. What good he has done is his own doing; if he brings ruin, he has only himself to blame. Such a mindset reflects what is commonly called humanism.

In today's world, there is nothing surprising in the statement, "I am a humanist." One could hear Hugh Hefner say these words and sense that they are congruent with the type of hedonism he has championed. Yet we would realize that the humanism of Hefner is a world away from the classical ideal of the Golden Mean, and that his type of humanism is hardly humane—to women or to men. Still, the confession, "I am a humanist," might come from a university professor of philosophy, a flower child at the airport, or a Marxist on the stump.

However, when an acknowledged evangelical theologian of the stature of J. I. Packer, author of the book *Knowing God,* says, "I am a humanist," then we must take notice. Either this stalwart of the faith is in the process of defection from his own confession, or there is another meaning to the word "humanism" than is usually found in the popular Christian press.

When we listen to Packer's full statement, we sense its audacity even more strongly: "I am a humanist. In truth, I believe it is only a thoroughgoing Christian who can ever have a right to that name."[1] These are bold, arresting words.

Moreover, I believe they represent the only defensible position for one who is committed to a biblical view of man as the special creation of God. I further believe this is the only view of man that fully takes into account the implications of the Incarnation of the Savior. For these reasons, we need to contrast the competing ideas of humanism in our age. There is a humanism that is false—damnably so. There is also a humanism that is true—theistic humanism which should be adopted anew by God's people.

Humanism—A Volatile Term

We may first note the false humanism that is so prevalent today. The notion of humanism has had a very long history, ranging from the classical periods of Greek and Roman times through the early centuries of the Renaissance in Europe and down to the many forms of humanism of our own day. A basic tenet of early humanism was expressed by the Latin writer Torence: "I am a man, and nothing human is foreign to me." In this view, the proper study of man is man himself.

Nightingale of the Muses

The sentiment, "Man is the measure of all things," is usually attributed to Protagoras, the fifth-century B.C. Greek sophist. Protagoras became an early victim of religious censorship for the beliefs he expressed in a daring new book on theology. The first sentence of the book expressed its thesis, and Protagoras's trouble:

> In regard to the gods I cannot know that they exist, nor yet that they do not exist; for many things hinder such knowledge—the obscurity of the matter, and the shortness of human life.[2]

Because he had questioned the concept that the gods could be known on the basis of empirical knowledge (though he had not in fact made an outright denial of the existence of the gods), Protagoras was accused of impiety. His book was banned and he was in danger of a court trial. He fled Athens for Sicily, but was subsequently lost at sea. Euripides mourned his friend in his play *Palamedes* with the choral lament: "Ye have slain, O Greeks, / ye have slain the nightingale of the Muses, / the wizard bird that do no wrong."[3]

Secular Humanism

The ancient concept that man is the measure of all things is a suitable premise for a contemporary materialist or atheist. While there are many forms of humanism in our day, the expression of humanism that most people think of is that called secular humanism. Robert Webber, professor of theology at Wheaton College, has presented a fine survey of the basic ideas of this movement in his book, *Secular Humanism: Threat and Challenge*. Among the items he discusses is the formal statement drafted in October 1980 by Paul Kurtz, editor of *The Humanist*, and signed by sixty-one scholars. The statement develops ten major tenets of contemporary secular humanism:

- free inquiry
- critical intelligence
- freedom
- evolution
- religious skepticism
- science and technology
- separation of church and state
- moral education
- knowledge through reason
- education[4]

Some of these planks in the humanist platform (freedom and education, for instance) might seem to be innocent in and of themselves, but Webber observes that in the humanist elaboration on each of these items, there is an attack on biblical faith.

> The most striking and recurring theme which runs through every point is that the church and Christianity are the enemy of the people and progress and that man himself has the capacity to save the world.[5]

These humanists are as opposed to communism as they are to the church, for they find both to be repressive to their concept of total freedom of inquiry. Christian ministers who attack secular humanists tend unfairly to link them with Russian communists, something not borne out by their literature.

The word "humanism" has become the new shibboleth, the new watchword, in some evangelical circles.[6] One who uses this word positively is in considerable danger of immediate judgment by the Jephthah's of our day. Blood still flows at the fords of the Jordan.

Humanism and Theism

The associations of the word humanism with pagan Greco-Roman culture, and with agnostic and atheistic proponents of our own day, make this term a surefire label for unbelief.

Once I was stopped at an airport by an activist with a clipboard wishing to enlist me in her cause. When I demurred, she asked, "Why won't you sign? If you are not for people, who are you for? What is there if there is not humanism?"

My first thought was to respond that there was theism. But on reflection, I realized that a proper view of theism demands humanism. What kind of theism would it be if man were held in low regard?—perhaps the type of theism against which Protagoras first objected, the sort found in pagan cultures throughout history.

Lord of the Flies

Certainly in the world of the ancient Near East one regularly had to contend with gods who were malevolent and with views of mankind that were seriously flawed. Consider the Babylonian narrative (which includes the parallel to the biblical story) of the great flood. In this account, *The Epic of Gilgamesh*, the reader finds a detestable concept of deity and a pitiable view of mankind.

At the end of the account of the flood, the Babylonian hero Utnapishtim builds an altar for the ravenously hungry gods, who had forgotten their own needs in their rash decision to destroy man by a great flood. They had decreed the end of mankind because their heavenly siestas were being disturbed by man's midday noises. The god Enlil had said, "The uproar of mankind is intolerable and sleep is no longer possible by reason of the babel." In their desire for rest, the gods had forgotten that it is clamorous men who feed them by sacrifice. When Utnapishtim debarked from the ark, the first thing he did was to offer a sacrifice to the deities of heaven.

> I made a sacrifice and poured out a libation on the mountain top. Seven and again seven cauldrons I set up on their stands, I heaped up wood and cane and cedar and myrtle. When the gods smelled the sweet savour, they gathered like flies over the sacrifice.[7]

The inspiration for William Golding's famous title, *Lord of the Flies,* ultimately comes from this scene. Golding's dark view of human nature has correspondence in the dark powers that animate them. Clamorous, but necessary men; hungry and fly-like gods—these are ideals one sometimes encounters in the literature of the ancient world.

A Heavenly Voyeur

In the religion of ancient Canaan, which came under the severe judgment of Yahweh, man was also presented in a debased manner and the gods were rarely praiseworthy. The god Baal, for example, is sometimes described in texts of such nastiness that the late William Foxwell Albright described the religious system of Canaan as the most depraved in history. Imagine worshiping a deity who is a celestial Peeping Tom, whose libido needs stimulating as he watches his devotees engaging in all manner of licentious, orgastic rites. Then, when fully aroused, he engages in sexual congress with the deities of the heavens, bringing about fertility on the earth. At times he disguises himself as a bull and attacks and rapes unwary women. The bull continues to be a transcultural symbol of overt sexuality, from the bullrings of Spain to the malt beer ads of American television.

Gilgamesh as Everyman

These things can be overstated, however. The story of Gilgamesh is essentially humanist. "Although the gods play a great part in the Epic, in its later form at least, *Gilgamesh* appears to have been as much a secular poem as the *Odyssey*."[8] The moral of the story is that one cannot live this life in fruitless pursuit of immortality. One should learn to enjoy the life one has. This is a basic humanistic point of view. There is a sense in which *Gilgamesh* may be read as the story of Everyman in search of meaning in life.

Condescending Baal

As we have noted, the gods of the ancient Near East were evil, untrustworthy, capricious, and petty. Rarely do the gods of the Canaanite pantheon present themselves in an attractive manner. One example is in a text of great poetic beauty from ancient Ugarit (an important city in northern Syria) that describes the power of Baal, the storm and fertility deity:

> I have a report I will relate to you
> an account I will repeat to you;
>> a report of a forest
>> and a whisper of a rock,
>>> A conversation of heavens to earth,
>>> of the ocean deep to the very stars:
>> I create lightning not comprehended by heavens;
>> a report which is not known by mankind,
>> nor understood by the multitudes of the earth.[9]

Peter C. Craigie comments on the loveliness of this ancient poetic text:

> Much of Ugaritic poetry is more impressive for its epic and narrative force than for the sheer literary beauty of its lines and words; but sometimes the Ugaritic poets achieved poetry that is remarkable in its own right.[10]

Again, while these words concerning Baal are descriptive of a putative deity in the rugged and wicked world of Canaanite mythology, there is something about these words that elicits a humanist response. Not only is there beauty of expression in these words, there is in them something of grace and condescension: a god is about to share with man something that man cannot know. In this stooping of deity, there is an elevating of the dignity of man. This is an altogether too rare illustration from a very pagan literature of what is regularly (and truly) encountered in the Bible.

Humanism—A Biblical View

In humanism there is a high view of the dignity and importance of man. Secular humanism sees that dignity and importance to be inherent in man apart from any consideration of deity. In contrast, biblical humanism affirms that man has great dignity and supreme importance because of the reality of who God is as Creator, Savior, and Judge, and what he does for his people based on these realities. That is, by virtue of the fact that God is described by what he does for man, there is a corresponding elevation of the dignity of man. As with the beautiful but rare description of Baal's condescension for the good of man (an aberration!), Yahweh is the stooping Deity of reality. The Scriptures are replete with examples.

The Sabbath and the Value of Man

The Lord Jesus went out of his way to demonstrate the high value of man in the estimation of God the Creator, whom he had come to explain (John 1:18). H. D. McDonald has discovered a splendid example of this factor:

> In a series of comparisons Jesus gave the clearest expression to his regard for man as a creature of the highest value. He contrasted man with the most cherished institutions of his day. There was no custom so firmly established and so fiercely defended at the time of Jesus than that of Sabbath-keeping. That which had been designed for man's good had become his master, its gracious purpose lost and its pleasures gone. Christ sought to shake man free from

the shackles of custom and to teach him that no institution has the worth of the human life for which it was instituted. The sabbath was made for man and not man for the sabbath (Mark 2:27; cf. Matthew 12:10f). . . . *Man has supreme value*. This is the first and most important truth that can be deduced from Christ's statements about the treatment of man. Each and every man is, *coram deo*, a creature of infinite worth.[11]

The words of Jesus that man is more important than the sabbath are sometimes interpreted as an example of the superiority of the freedom of the New Testament faith over the legalistic constraints of the Old Testament. Jesus is viewed as a revolutionary who saw truths in the biblical tradition that had never been seen before his time. A proper view both of Christ and of the Scripture is to find in him the true interpreter of the text, not a revolutionary who imported meaning that was never there.

Ruth the Alien

In the little Book of Ruth, just as in the teaching of the Lord Jesus, we find another biblical example of the supreme importance of man over institutions. Jesus' approach to the sabbath finds its analogue in the reception of Ruth the Moabitess in the community of Israel.

I suspect that many readers of the Book of Ruth would be surprised to learn the nature of the legal status of Moabites in Israel. But the legislation in Deuteronomy 23:3-6 has major significance in our reading of the story of Ruth and Naomi. The fact is this: Moabites were excluded from the congregation of Israel for ten generations. That is, if a proselyte were to come to saving faith in Yahweh, it was expected that his or her descendants would be excluded from full participation in the community for an exceedingly lengthy period. In fact, the Bible may imply an exclusion of Moabites from Israel in perpetuity.[12]

The reason for this exclusion is clear. Since Moab did not

meet Israel with friendliness as they journeyed out of Egypt, but hired Balaam in a vain attempt to destroy Israel by a divine curse, Moab was placed under a spiritual interdict: "Do not seek peace or good relations with them as long as you live" (Deuteronomy 23:6).

Yet in the lovely story of Ruth, we have a Moabitess who is accepted into the congregation fully and immediately. Her expressions of loyal love both to her dead husband and to her mother-in-law Naomi are noteworthy in an age of general impiety among the people of the covenant. Further, her own confession of faith in Yahweh (Ruth 1:16; 2:11-12) was deep, genuine, and lasting.

Ruth was from a culture believed to be totally alien to Israel. But because of the excellence of her faith in Yahweh and her nobility of character, she was given the blessing of the matriarchs by the townspeople of Bethlehem (Ruth 4:11-12), and she herself was judged to be of greater worth than the son she bore (Ruth 4:14-16). In just a few generations her line led to David, the great king of Israel (Ruth 4:18-21), and ultimately to Jesus the Messiah (Matthew 1:5, 16).

This is extraordinary. The Bible presents a stern regulation against a wicked nation because of its perfidy against Israel in the days of her youth. Yet one woman from that nation, because of her loyal love and piety toward Yahweh, the Lord of Israel, was made an exception. In both Testaments the value of the human being who responds to God may transcend even the normal expectations of the ordinances of God.

As we shall see in chapter 8, one issue in the Scriptures demonstrates this truth far beyond the illustrations we have just noted. The final and convincing evidence of the humanism of Scripture is seen in an appreciation of the full implications of the Incarnation. For it is by means of the Incarnation that God himself became Man—the supreme demonstration of his value of the human person.

Instead of fleeing from humanism because of what we perceive to be its negative meaning, or instead of developing a subbiblical view of man as a reaction to the overestimation of man given by nontheistic humanists, the call to the true believer in Jesus is a call to theistic humanism. We need to relearn the estimation of man given by the Scriptures.

The alternative to the religious right and religious left is the recovery of an authentic Christian humanism.[13]

Chapter 4, Notes

1. J. I. Packer, *Knowing Man* (Westchester, Ill.: Crossway Books, 1979), 11.

2. Cited by J. B. Bury, *A History of Greece to the Death of Alexander the Great* (reprint, New York: The Modern Library, n.d.), 371.

3. Ibid.

4. Robert E. Webber, *Secular Humanism: Threat and Challenge* (Grand Rapids: Zondervan Publishing House, 1982), 37-47.

5. Ibid., 47.

6. See Judges 12:4-6.

7. N. K. Sandars, trans., *The Epic of Gilgamesh* (Baltimore: Penguin Books, 1960), 108-9.

8. Ibid., 30.

9. The translation of this poem (ʿnt III:17-25) is my own, but I am indebted to Peter C. Craigie for stressing its beauty and for his suggestion of the translation "I create" instead of "I understand" for the verb *'abn.* See Peter C. Craigie, *Ugarit and the Old Testament* (Grand Rapids: Wm. B. Eerdmans Publishing Co., 1983), 53-54.

10. Ibid., 54.

11. H. D. McDonald, *The Christian View of Man,* in *Foundations for Faith,* ed. Peter Toon (Westchester, Ill.: Crossway Books, 1981), 2.

12. See Peter C. Craigie, *The Book of Deuteronomy, The New International Commentary on the Old Testament* (Grand Rapids: Wm. B. Eerdmans Publishing Co., 1976), 297.

13. Webber, *Secular Humanism,* 16.

PART 2

THE MAJESTY OF MAN

David asks that question with a holy wonder,
Quid est homo? *What is man that God is so mindful of
him? But I may have his leave, and the holy Ghost's,
to say, since God is so mindful of him, since God hath
set his mind upon him, What is not man?*
Man is all.
*Since we consider men in the place that they hold,
and value them according to those places, and ask not
how they got thither, when we see Man made
The Love of the Father, The Price of the Son,
The Temple of the Holy Ghost, The Signet upon God's
hand, The Apple of God's eye, Absolutely,
unconditionally we cannot annihilate man, not
evacuate, not evaporate, not extenuate man* . . . .

*For man is not only a contributary Creature,
but a total Creature; He does not only make one,
but he is all; He is not a piece of the world,
but the world itself; and next to the glory of God,
the reason why there is a world.*
John Donne
"First Prebend Sermon"
8 May 1625

Chapter 5

In Praise of Man

While I was in graduate school, I worked for a couple of years as an announcer on a classical radio station. I had had no formal training in radio, but I had a great love for music and was able to pass the audition for voice quality and the ability to pronounce the names of composers and performers.

However, my career in radio nearly came to an early and abrupt end. On my second night I was scheduled to play the entire *Messiah* by Handel. What a feast of music that night was to be! It was only after the music had begun that the evening turned sour for me. I found that at 9:00 P.M. in addition to giving the normal station break, I was to play an advertisement for a health product of a very personal nature before returning to the *Messiah*. Now I am certain that many people have a bodily complaint for which this medication may be of relief. But I simply could not bring myself to play the taped promo for "Preparation H" in the middle of the *Messiah*. There are some things that simply do not belong together! I was pretty sure that my job was on the line, but I wrote a note on my log saying that I just could not bring myself to play that ignoble ad in the middle of that sublime music.

As it turned out, the station manager himself nearly had a fit when he read his own log in his office later that evening. The ad had been placed there by error. He was saved from apoplexy when he learned that I had not in fact played the promo. "Some things just do not belong together," he said. In the middle of some of the most glorious music ever created by man in praise of God, there is simply no place for certain types of commerce.

I assert that the phrase "secular humanism" is as unfortunate a coupling of ideas as an ad for a personal health remedy in the middle of the *Messiah*. Humanism ought not to be seen in a secular context but in its proper biblical frame, the praise of God. Humanism—properly understood—does not belong to those who have no room for the Creator. Only with a high view of God may one have a proper view of man. As we shall see, such is the explicit teaching of the eighth Psalm.

The Frame of Praise to God

Psalm 8 is a particular favorite of many readers of the Old Testament hymns. One of the things that makes this Psalm compelling is its structure. The Psalm begins and ends with the same words of praise to God:

> O LORD, our Lord,
> how majestic is your name in all the earth!

These words speak with awe and wonder of the glory of God. They are in tune with the dominant notion of the Book of Psalms: the proper response to Yahweh is the praise of his people. An attentive reader will observe that two terms are used of God in the phrasing, "O LORD, our Lord." "LORD" is the name of God in the Hebrew Bible—Yahweh. By this name the Blessed One asserts both his sublime existence as well as his relatedness to his people. The One who says of himself "I AM" (Exodus 3:14) is the One who forever is for his people. The term "our Lord" speaks of his sovereignty as well as his relatedness to his people. At the very thought of his name, the psalmist declares: "How majestic in all the earth!"

There is no question, then, that this Psalm is strongly theistic. Having these words of praise to God at the beginning and the end of the poem provides a specific frame for the poem. That frame is the praise of God.

What Then Is Man?

But the central picture of the Psalm is the praise of man. That man may be praised in the context of the praise of God is the startling teaching of this poem, and the thesis of this book.

We are all familiar with the basic question of this Psalm. It is the question that all of us likely have asked at one time or another: In view of the vastness of the universe, what is man in the sight of God? If there is a Creator of all that exists, is it even rational to think that he should be concerned about me?

> When I consider your heavens,
>   the work of your fingers,
> the moon and the stars,
>   which you have set in place,
> what is man that you are mindful of him,
>   the son of man that you care for him?
>   (Psalm 8:3-4)

Man and Space

Here is an issue that calls for balance. Man tends to think either too highly or not highly enough of himself. Writer and Bible teacher David Needham relates how he drove one winter from the wet and rainy Portland area to the eastern part of Oregon where he could dry out and see the stars again. He found a place where he could roll out his mat and sleeping bag; then he crawled in to watch the stars and, as he put it, "to contemplate my smallness." Such reflection mirrors the spirit of David as he thinks of himself in the context of the vastness of space. These words call for humility.

And how vast is space? Current scientific theory estimates that the universe is seventeen billion light years across. (Did you think it was nearer eighteen?) I have no capacity to imagine such a distance; such vastness is quite too much for me. When I think of the universe and then think of myself, I must be truly humbled.

Not Such Big Stuff

Each spring I present a number of Passover *seders*. During the beautiful and significant feast, I ask the men to wear *yarmulkas* as Jewish men do in a similar service. I am always asked why we wear these little "beanies." So I asked a rabbi friend to explain to me the significance of the *yarmulka*.

He said, "Do you want me to explain the meaning of the *yarmulka?*"

I responded that I did indeed.

"All right. I'll tell you."

I waited.

After a pause he said, "We don't know."

He did speak of tradition. Then he offered a number of explanations. The one that I liked the best is that the *yarmulka* is like the palm of the hand of God resting in blessing on the man in the home saying, "Little man, you're not such big stuff!"

This is the case indeed. The universe is the creation of God. Yahweh has made it all. To the Creator we sing, the heavens are "your heavens," the universe is "the work of your fingers." As the crafting of a modeler or the stitching of a seamstress, so the cosmos is the finger work of Almighty God.

And what is man in all of that? In view of the universe, is it even reasonable to assume that man is any more than a rash on the epidermis of the earth? Is not man just a dust-particled creature on a little planet in a backward part of the universe? What is man? The question is familiar to all of us. It is the answer that is startling.

Greater Than Angels

The response of the psalmist to the question "What is man?" is so surprising that many readers both ancient and modern have stumbled over these words. The familiar words of the King James Version read:

> For thou hast made him a little lower
>   than the angels,
> and hast crowned him with glory and honour.
> (Psalm 8:5)

While it is true that this translation is well-established in the King James tradition (witness the New King James Version), as well as in the New Testament citation in Hebrews 2 (which we will examine in a later chapter), in point of fact the expression "a little lower than the angels" is not the clear reading of the Hebrew text. The reading is very old, however. The antecedents to the interpretation of this verse go back to the Septuagint, the ancient Jewish translation of the Hebrew Bible into Greek.

The rendering "angels" for the Hebrew term '*elohim* seems to have been a desperate attempt on the part of the translators of the Septuagint to avoid what they determined to be a difficulty in their own culture. Had they translated "a little lower than God," would not their pagan neighbors accuse them of worshiping demigods? Where would the great Jewish declaration of monotheism go if they admitted to this high view of man? Yet in our culture, we need the bold pronouncement of the text to be given clearly. In our day it is the nature of man that needs to be clarified.

Here is a more literal reading of verse 5:

> But you have caused him to lack
> but little of God;
> and with glorious honor,
> you have crowned him.[1]

The audacity of this text will not go away. In response to the question, "What is man?" comes an answer of majesty: Man is made a little lower than God and is crowned by him with glory and honor. It is in the context of the praise of God that man has his true meaning and dignity.

Man—God's "8" or "9"

It is not that we are lower than the angels. In fact, for man to desire to be like an angel is to desire a lower order than God has made him to be. Donne states the matter well: "yet man cannot deliberately wish himself an Angel, because he should lose by that wish, and lack that glory, which he shall have in his body."[2]

Instead of the expected response that man is frightfully

insignificant to God, this Psalm insists that man is of immense importance to God. "If one were to imagine a scale of 1 to 10 with living creatures such [as] beasts at 1 and God at 10, then, so high is the writer's estimate of man, one should have to put him at 8 or 9."[3]

And what is it that prompts David to make such a bold statement? It is the biblical view of creation.

> You made him ruler over the works of your hands;
>   you put everything under his feet:
> all flocks and herds,
>   and the beasts of the field,
> the birds of the air,
>   and the fish of the sea,
>   all that swim the paths of the seas.
> (Psalm 8:6-8)

Back to Moses

The mention of man as regent of God over flocks, herds, beasts, birds, fish, and swimming things draws us strongly to the source of David's thoughts, back to the creation text in Genesis 1 where these very concepts were first given (1:26-28).

As he thought of stars and moon above and of his own place in the universe, David realized anew that he—as man— was the centerpiece of God's work. Man is the apex of creation, the chef d'oeuvre of God—God's masterpiece! After God had made all that he made, then God made man. And when he made man it was in his own image. The expression of David, "You have made him a little lower than God" (Psalm 8:5), is a poetic reflection of the statement of Moses, "God created man in his own image" (Genesis 1:27).

With the words of the Psalm in mind, listen again to the familiar refrain of Genesis 1:26-28:

> Then God said, "Let us make man in our image, in our likeness, and let them rule over the fish of the sea and the birds of the air, over the livestock, over all the earth, and over all the creatures that move along the ground."

So God created man in his own image,
in the image of God he created him;
male and female he created them.

God blessed them and said to them, "Be fruitful and increase in number; fill the earth and subdue it. Rule over the fish of the sea and the birds of the air and over every living creature that moves on the ground."

There can be little doubt that David's poem is based upon this section of the Bible. To man, a creature of seeming insignificance, God has given great dignity. To man, little and lost in the vastness of space, God has given sovereignty. To man, puny and restless and weak, God has given a part of himself. Of all God's creatures, only man is made in his image. Man is the crown of the cosmos, the measure of creation. Man as male and female is God's finest work.

True Dignity

It is in the context of a strong belief in the Creator and in his creation that man finds his true dignity.

Man's dignity rests in God who assigns an inestimable worth to every person. Man's origin is not an accident, but a profoundly intelligent act by One who has eternal value; by One who stamps His own image on each person. God creates men and moves heaven and earth to redeem them when they fall. Our origin is in creation and our destiny is for redemption. Between these points every human heartbeat has value.[4]

Fallenness and Wonders

It is also in the context of a strong belief in the Creator and in his creation that I as a Christian can gain a new perspective on the things that man is able to do as he fulfills the mandate to rule as the regent of God. We need to realize that David's words do not ignore the fact of fallenness; they are written in full cognizance of the reality of sin in man. Verse 2 of Psalm 8 speaks of the enemies of God. But, wonderfully, this Psalm says that from man in his frailest state may come words of praise that will confound all enemies of God:

> From the lips of children and infants
> you have ordained praise[5]
> because of your enemies,
> to silence the foe and the avenger.
>
> (Psalm 8:2)

Man is fallen, but man may still do wonders as he fulfills God's mandate to rule over creation. The believer is able to respond to the wonders of man and give praise to God, thus silencing the enemy and realizing the very goal of creation. This is the point of Psalm 8 as we can see once again in the last verse:

> O LORD, our Lord,
> how majestic is your name in all the earth!
>
> (Psalm 8:9)

These words provide not only the structural cohesion that ties the Psalm together, they point to the theology of this poem: When we have a right view of man we will be led to a new praise of God.

A Golden Wonder

Not long ago my wife Beverly and I came to realize these truths in a new and dramatic way through several incidents that came in a cluster. We had a ministry in northern California with adults from five Chinese churches in the San Francisco Bay area. As we were driving back to "the City" with Pastor and Mrs. Benjamin Wong, we began to talk about the Golden Gate Bridge. Pastor Wong told us he would like us to have a new view of that bridge. As we neared the northern entrance to the bridge, he turned the car west, up a winding dirt road on army property to a very high point from which we looked down on the bay and the bridge. It was just at the time of sunset on a particularly beautiful winter day. All was awash in reds and purples and oranges, the sun seemingly slipping into the sea.

We said nothing—we just looked. We looked at the wonder of God in the beauty of the bay. We looked at the wonder of man in the beauty of the bridge. Bay and bridge joined hands—both spoke of beauty and wonder. There it was! In the beauty of that bridge, man has given praise to God his creator.

Later when we were on the bridge, Pastor Wong asked if we had heard about the recent closing of the Golden Gate because of high winds. We had. He related that the winds were blowing so strongly that the bridge was moving some eight feet from its normal placement. The bridge was closed, however, not because of any danger that might come to it, but because of the fear drivers would experience on the moving structure. They had paid to cross the bridge and found themselves at Marriott's Great America. But the bridge was built to withstand not eight feet of movement, we were told, but twenty-eight feet!

This is truly a marvel. In the beauty and the strength and stability of that bridge, man has truly done a wonder. Some look at the bridge and see in it only a mark of the genius of man. Writer Cliff Tarpy, for example, speaks of the bridge in glowing terms:

> Some say San Francisco is the most feminine city in the world. If so, the Golden Gate Bridge is the matriarch. I could see that exquisite marriage of form and function from my hotel window. The curve of the cables between her two 746-foot towers was the smile of a woman who in her 44 years has seen it all.[6]

I concur with these expressions. But I would add that there is something in the excellence of this structure that should call for praise to God for the Christian who beholds it. That is, God should be praised for what he has enabled man to do. We came to this conclusion on the basis of our experience that night. Only later did a Christian woman in the Bay area give me a religious tract written by the designer of the bridge, stating his intention that the bridge glorify God. My point would be true even if we did not have this happy news. Yet how very sad it is when a person who has come to the end of hope goes out on that bridge on a foggy night and casts himself into the waters below. Some people can look at the bridge and not see it at all. Others look at the bridge and see only the work of man.

The Sand Cries Out

After we returned to our home I turned in my grades. Since I was a day late (as is too often the case), I went rather sheepishly to the registrar's office to turn them in for processing. Despite myself, I smiled again at the majesty of man as the records clerk began to record my grades.

A few years ago there was a major project to bring computer technology to the seminary. A large room was prepared in the basement of the men's dorm: subflooring was put in, air conditioning was installed, the room was filled with all manner of mysterious whirring equipment, and a staff was assembled to keep it all running. Then a few years later we got rid of all that whirring junk and acquired a desk top minicomputer that was able to process more data more quickly than the entire room full of equipment. Now, with a mainframe unit, the school is in a different world.

The silicon chip is a marvel. It is a genuine wonder of what man is able to do as he fulfills the mandate God has given him to rule over creation. The words of Genesis 1 and Psalm 8 concerning man's dominion over nature do not end with animal training! Listen again to the words of Psalm 8:6:

> You made him ruler over the works of your hands;
> you put everything under his feet.

Man is not only able to construct a magnificent bridge of metal, he is able to make of a piece of sand a technological marvel that may be used in nearly every area of human endeavor. The silicon chip is a triumph of the human imagination. It is a tribute to the ingenious use man has made of the elements of the earth that God has provided him. As I write these words on a computer in my own home, it is with a prayer of praise to God who has brought me to such an age. In the wonders of man there is new reason to give praise to God.

Dickens and Gospel

Then, with grades in, Beverly and I were able to watch on television (another wonder) the four-evening production of the classic by Charles Dickens, *Nicholas Nickleby,* performed by the Royal Shakespeare Company.

We watched with deep emotion the touching scene where Nicholas awakens after he has fled Dotheboys Hall, that terrible home for boys, because of countless acts of inhumanity. Nicholas had slept in a barn. When he woke up he found Smike at his feet. Smike—that pitiable boy, twisted and tormented— had never been treated like a human being except once in his life, and that was when he was accorded human dignity by Nicholas.

Nicholas asked Smike why he was kneeling before him. The wretched lad replied:

> "To go with you—anywhere—everywhere—to the world's end—to the churchyard grave," replied Smike, clinging to his hand. "Let me, oh do let me. You are my home—my kind friend—take me with you, pray."[7]

The emotion of friendship, the sense of dependence, the spirit of dignity—all were likely designed by Dickens to point to the story of the gospel. I could not but be moved by these words to give praise to God. I was intrigued to learn that I am not alone in this response. At the end of her Introduction to this novel, Dame Sybil Thorndike, who sees Christian motifs throughout the book, concludes: "Praise the Lord for Charles Dickens!"[8] Amen.

The Dark Side

This view of the wonders that man may do in praise of God is not presented in ignorance of the wickedness of man—no more so than to suggest that David was unaware of man's wickedness when he wrote Psalm 8. We are well aware that man, who can design a bridge of exquisite beauty, may also design an instrument of terrible cruelty. The silicon chip, which may be used to run a seminary or write a book, may be used as well in programming instruments of destruction that may endanger civilization itself. A man who may write a book of worth and lasting literary quality may also write himself and his readers damned.

We shall say more of evil. Here we wish to speak of good. When you next see something that man has done that is true, noble, right, pure, lovely, admirable, excellent, or praiseworthy, then think about these things. And in your thoughts—and in your words—reflect on the wonder of God who has given such wonders to man!

A proper picture of man is found in the frame of the praise of Yahweh.

Chapter 5, Notes

1. Personal translation. The New American Standard Bible reads, "Yet Thou hast made him a little lower than God, / And dost crown him with glory and majesty!" The New International Version seems to straddle the fence by reading, "You made him a little lower than the heavenly beings / and crowned him with glory and honor." "Heavenly beings" seems to be some kind of compromise between "God" and "angels." All authorities agree that the expected and regular translation of the term *'elohim* is *God* (or *gods,* when used of pagan deities). The margin of the NIV notes: "Or *than God.*"

2. John Donne, "First Prebend Sermon," preached at St. Paul's, 8 May 1625, in *Donne's Prebend Sermons,* ed. Janel M. Mueller (Cambridge, Mass.: Harvard University Press, 1971), 77. Spellings have been changed to conform to current practice.

3. Elmer A. Martens, *God's Design: A Focus on Old Testament Theology* (Grand Rapids: Baker Book House, 1981), 164. When Martens goes on to say, "The psalmist is not a humanist," he doubtless is speaking of secular humanism, and not against the view espoused in this book.

4. R. C. Sproul, *In Search of Dignity* (Ventura, Calif.: Regal Books, 1983), 94.

5. The translation "praise" in verse 2 in the NIV is unexpected, but is likely the correct intention of the term (c.f., "strength" in KJV, NASB; "bulwark" in RSV).

6. Cliff Tarpy, "The Beauty and the Battles of San Francisco Bay," *National Geographic* (June 1981), 844.

7. Charles Dickens, *The Life and Adventures of Nicholas Nickleby,* 2 vols., The Centennial Edition (Geneva: Heron Books, n.d.), 1:192.

8. Ibid., xvi.

*Last Shabbos there began one of those well intended
but empty exchanges that sometimes populate the
minutes of rabbis after a service. I said to a man,
"Where are you from?" He said, "I don't know."
(Just what I needed, an existentialist.) "C'mon, where
are you from?" But again he insisted that he did not
know. I looked more closely and saw that he was not
an amnesia victim, a junkie, or an alcoholic. He was
simply a human being who was moved by our worship
experience and who had come forward. "Where are
you from, Rabbi?" And then I realized what was
going on and what I had learned. I told him that I
didn't know where I was from either. For I understood
then that I didn't. "In that case you understand what
I'm trying to say," he said. And I did. And we parted.*
Lawrence Kushner
Honey from the Rock (D'Vash MiSela):
Visions of Jewish Mystical Renewal

*Man is so the universe will have something to talk
through, so God will have something to talk with, and
so the rest of us will have something to talk about.*
Frederick Buechner
Wishful Thinking: A Theological ABC

Chapter 6

In His Image

*I*n the first chapter we asked the question, "Whither man?" That is, Where is man going in these latter years of the twentieth century? In this chapter we ask the complements, "Whence man, and for what?" That is, Where did man come from and for what purpose does he exist?

Where Are You From?

The words Rabbi Kushner asked his visitor in the story at the beginning of this chapter are common enough, but more than one thing may be meant by them. "Where are you from?" can be used as a casual gambit in a synagogue or a single's bar; or it may lead one to a new mystical reality or a deep metaphysical discussion. But for the biblically oriented believer, these words lead one finally back to Moses and the Law, to words that describe man's very beginning and that point out man's true origin. Further, more is involved in the reason for man than is suggested by the imaginative theologian Frederick Buechner.

One of the most amazing wonders of the nature and purpose of man is that these questions and their answers are revealed by the Creator himself. We are not left to our own devices.

From the Heart of God

We may begin by asserting that man originates from the very heart of God. German theologian Gerhard von Rad bases this point of view on the creation story in Genesis:

> We have, therefore, an ascending line; at the tip of the pyramid is man, for he alone of all creatures is the closest to God. His creation alone is preceded by a solemn decision in God's heart: "Let us make man in our image." Only man, therefore, owes his existence to a voluntary decision in the depths of God's heart.[1]

Not only is man created by the decision of the heart of God, he is made in the divine image. It is precisely this—man fashioned in the image of God—that makes the concept of the majesty of man biblically appropriate. Man's majesty is derived from his intimate association with the Creator.

> Every relationship to God in the world is thus summed up in man. In him the world has its most direct connection to God; no creature is closer to God than he. Before God he is the center and goal of creation.[2]

The Decision of God

In the last chapter we learned that David wrote Psalm 8 in conscious reflection upon Genesis 1:26-28. It is on this foundation text that our own understanding of man must be based. These three verses of majestic prose and elevated poetry speak of the finest of the works of God: his fashioning of man. Here are the words of that text in a personal rendering:

> (26) Then God said,
>   "Let us make man in our image,
>   according to our likeness;
>   and let them rule over the fish of the sea,
>   and over the birds of the heavens,
>   and over the larger animals,
>   even over all the earth,
>   and over all the smaller creatures
>   which move about over the earth."

(27) So God created man in his image,
In the image of God he created him;
Male and female he created them.

(28) And God blessed them,
And God said to them:
"Be fruitful and multiply,
And fill the earth and subdue it;
And rule over the fish of the sea,
and over the birds of the heavens,
and over every living thing that moves
about on the earth."

A Verbal Pyramid

The structure of Genesis 1 is climactic. After God had made everything else, he then was ready for his masterwork. Only after he had called into being the entire universe was God prepared to create the creature who would proceed from his own heart and with whom he would have conversation. This creature is man.

The structure of Genesis 1:26-28 is pyramidal. Verses 26 and 28, with their similar sections on the rule of man over the rest of God's creatures, serve as the twin bases for the triangle's peak in the central verse. Further, verses 26 and 28 are poetic prose; verse 27 is pure poetry. This structure may be visualized as follows:

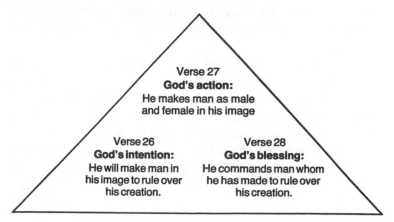

The Structure of Recital

As we have already indicated, verse 27 is finely crafted poetry. It is composed of a tricolon (a three line unit) with synonymous parallelism. The meter of the verse is finely balanced; in the original text each line has four beats or accented words. Further, each of the three lines uses the Hebrew verb *bara'*, "He created." The three-fold use of this verb of divine activity is noteworthy. It calls attention to itself. Only in two other verses of Genesis 1 does this verb appear. It is used at the very beginning in the summary statement of verse 1: "In the beginning God created (*bara'*) the heavens and the earth." The same verb is then used in verse 21 of God's creation of the creatures of the sea and the birds of the air. But in verse 27, *bara'* is found in each member of the three-fold poetic declaration of the creation of man.

This elevated repetition of language is for emphasis and for emotional and aesthetic effects. According to the late Jewish scholar Umberto Cassuto,

> The poetic structure of the sentence [of verse 27], its stately diction and its particular emotional quality attest the special importance that the Torah attributes to the making of man—the noblest of the creatures.[3]

Out of Nothing?

At times one hears remarks made about the meaning of *bara'* that are misleading. It is commonly assumed, for example, that the precise meaning of *bara'* is "to create out of nothing."[4]

We do not wish to deny that the ultimate creative act of God was to bring matter "out of nothing." This is the teaching of Hebrews 11:3, and is the essence of biblical faith: "By faith we understand that the universe was formed at God's command, so that what is seen was not made out of what was visible."

The association of a belief in the ultimate creation of matter and the basic concept of biblical faith is to be maximized, not minimized in our living. An ancient, and still relevant, statement of Christian confession begins with these words of affirmation: "I believe in God the Father Almighty, Maker of heaven and earth." It is truly unfortunate that evangelical churches who do believe in God's creative work do not vocalize their confession in community recital. What loss we suffer when we ignore the biblical, apostolic, and historic practice of the recital of the creeds together in our worship. We who believe in creation should affirm that belief in our worship, not just in debates with college sophomores. Hebrews 11:3 calls for a recital of belief among God's people.[5]

Bara' and Out of Nothing

Our point is not that we should question the concept of the original creation by God out of nothing, but that we may not base this teaching solely upon the Hebrew verb *bara'*. A study of the word throughout the Old Testament (see Appendix) suggests that its consistent meaning is "to fashion anew—a divine activity." The creative activity of God described by *bara'* is a wonder that calls for the adoration of God by his people. When the creation of man is described, such a wonder is envisioned by Moses that he uses *bara'* three times in one verse.

Out of Something—a Wonder

The essential issue here is not that man was created out of nothing. As we know from Genesis 2:7, the male in fact was made from the dust of the ground and the female from the rib of man. In both the male and the female, God used preexisting material in his wonder-formation. The essential issue is that man was created by an act of God. It is wonder and newness that marks *bara'* in its three-fold use in Genesis 1:27. When God made man he made something entirely new in the created order.

Dietrich Bonhoeffer came to this conclusion a generation ago, although without particular reference to the meaning of the verb we have suggested:

> Man shall proceed from God as his ultimate, his new
> work, and as the image of God in his creation. There

is no transition here from somewhere or other, there is new creation. This has nothing to do with Darwinism: quite independently of this man remains the new, free, undetermined work of God.[6]

This view of man in dignity is not secular; it is theistic. This high conception of man as wonder is not antireligious; it is pure, revealed theology. Man is God's great wonder-work!

The Music of Restatement

Let's look again at those magnificent words in Genesis 1:27. We have already observed in this foundation text the factor of repetition:

> So God created man in his own image,
>   in the image of God he created him;
>   male and female he created them.

Parallelism—statement followed by restatement—is the genius of Hebrew poetry. It is the function of *synonymous parallelism,* such as is found here, not to be redundant but to state the same thought in slightly different words for a cumulative effect. This is neither bombast nor overkill; the creative manner in which Old Testament artists reworded parallel elements is the very thing that gives life and joy to Hebrew poetry.[7]

We might make a mistake in our reading of these words, thinking that each of the three elements is to be read independently of the other. But this would be a fragmentary approach to art, much like listening to contrasting melodies of contrapuntal music one at a time. Such a task might be undertaken by a person who desires to learn the parts before the whole, but if one does not go beyond this he is engaging in artistic nihilism. The effect desired by the composer will only be achieved when the two (or more) themes are heard together in concert, interplaying with one another in the magic of music. Similarly, we must hear the lines of parallel poetry as they interplay if we are to experience the effect the poet intended.

Let's first look briefly at the parts, and then we may hear them together. The first colon of Genesis 1:27 emphasizes that man is the creation of God. The second specifies more emphatically that as God's creation, man was fashioned in the divine image. The third line details that man, God's creation fashioned in the divine image, was created male and female.

It is only when all three channels of this verse are heard interplaying with each other that we may have the intended meaning of Torah. Let the parts resound together; listen to the music!

Male and Female

I am afraid there are those who have written on the concept of man in the image of God who are somewhat tone-deaf; they seem not to have heard all the orchestration of this tricolon. Man in the image of God has been limited to Adam too often. The Torah clearly expresses the fact that it is in man as male and female, man as Adam and Eve, that the image of God was realized.

Genesis 1:27 presents a triptych:

(1) Man is God's creation.
(2) Man is created in God's image.
(3) Man is created by God as male and female.[8]

This verse demands equality between the female and the male; male and female together are created in the image of God. I do not believe it is possible for a true biblical theology to be presented if this issue is muddled. There is no room in biblical thought that the female is worthy of any less dignity than the male. The concept of the image of God in man likely involves more than the male-female relationship; but it does embrace that relationship. We may not wish to walk the full distance of the road that Paul K. Jewett has taken, but we cannot ignore the signpost and roadmarker he has established:

If Man is male and female by the Creator's decision and act, so that *her* creation is in some sense the completion of *his* creation, then a theology of Man that is male-oriented is surely not one that is based on revelation, one that strives to think God's thoughts after him.[9]

Another Story, Another Issue

When we turn from Genesis 1 to Genesis 2, we find a different but complementary picture. What two poetic lines do in the microcosm, these two chapters do in a larger sphere—they too are to be heard together for the effect of Torah to be achieved.

When we read chapter 2 we learn something that was not stated in the first account. The male, Adam, was created before the female, Eve. Whereas Genesis 1 speaks of the equality of male and female as image-bearers of God, Genesis 2 presents a slight priority of the male over the female because of the order of creation. This priority does not destroy the equality; it conjoins with it.

When God's Work Was "Not Good"

Genesis 2:18-25 is the key passage for our discussion. It is here that we learn that the man who was alone was judged by God to be in a condition that was "not good." These extraordinary words run counter to the whole expectation of the first chapter where "good" was pronounced seven times. The male by himself is incomplete; he is in a condition that is not good. But later, when he is presented with his partner, created as the very complement to himself, the words "very good" are very much in order (Genesis 1:31).

Hence God declares his intention to fashion a helper corresponding exactly to the male and complementing him in every way (Genesis 2:18). The term "helper" is not a demeaning term; it is elsewhere used of God, who is also man's helper (Psalms 10:14; 54:4). The work the male was to do in response to the Creator's great commission was not a work he could do alone.

We may ask if man in solitude was made in God's image. Was Adam in God's image before there was an Eve? That is, is it possible for an individual to be an image-bearer, or does image-bearing demand the male-female complement? Recent writings in women's studies suggest that the image of God is to be defined specifically in terms of male-female. The apostle Paul, in reference to Genesis 2, seems to suggest that the male himself was made in the image of God (1 Corinthians 11:7-8).

The question is moot, however, for his solitude was not long-lived, and was "not good." Even Paul concludes that "woman is not independent of man, nor is man independent of woman"—in the Lord (1 Corinthians 11:11). I believe we may say that the man alone was made in God's image (and that the woman alone was made in God's image as well!), but that the command to be image-bearers is a task that must be accomplished together. Adam needed a partner, a helper thoroughly suited[10] to join hands in the task of being man, the wonder work of Yahweh.

All Creatures Great and Small

The Lord Yahweh then did an amazing thing. In order vividly to demonstrate to Adam the lack of a suitable helper among all God's variegated creatures—and to build in Adam an anticipation and an appreciation for God's coming gift—Yahweh God paraded before the man samples of all his creatures for the man to name.[11]

This naming of the animals was a complex function of an extraordinarily gifted man. Adam was not just giving the animals numbers (and certainly not beastly "grunts"); he was giving insightful names—names that would stick—to each of the animals God paraded before him. This text demands an intellectual and language ability on the part of our first parent that would be in accord with the design of the Creator.

Adam's superior intellect was clearly demonstrated by his ability to name every creature he saw. But in none of them did he find his complement.

> In Semitic thought, naming implied the ability to learn the inner secrets or essence of an object, just as man has such powers in science today. Man's power to so 'name' the animals was notably set in the context of his recognition of his own relational needs.[12]

Moreover, in giving a name to every creature, Adam was asserting his royal role of dominion. The Bible is explicit in affirming that to name someone or something is a "token of lordship" (see Numbers 32:38; 2 Kings 23:34; 24:17; 2 Chronicles 36:4; Daniel 1:6-7).

The Lord of the universe named the parts of the universe and its time-divisions [Genesis 1:5, 8, 10], and he left it to man to determine the names of those creatures over which he had given him dominion.[13]

The Hebrew verb "to name" is given in our text three times for emphasis. Adam was lord—but he was a lonely lord.

And Then There Was Woman

Finding no complement to himself, Adam became the subject of the first surgery in history. God is not only the Healer; he is the Surgeon as well. Bone (with attendant flesh)[14] was taken from Adam's side to stress that his helper was his counterpart. Yet the fact that he was created before the one being made of his own body gives him a certain sense of priority of relationship, a slight seniority of existence.

Whereas the text has implied the great gift of language in Adam—one of the major characteristics of humanity—it is not until Genesis 2:23 that the text actually reports his words. Significantly, we do not have Adam's words about birds, beasts, or fish; we have his words about woman. And in these words we are impressed with his intelligence, his tenderness, his insight—and his lordship. Adam recognizes in the woman his own counterpart. He is overjoyed at her fittingness. But he is the one who names her, just as he has given names to the animals and the birds. Yet look at the name he gives her—it is a name that mirrors his own. His naming of her is an expression of the compassionate lordship of an equal.

> This one! This time!
> (That is, At last!—here is one who
> corresponds directly and truly to me!)
> Bone—from my bones!
> And flesh—from my flesh!
> This one shall be called woman,
> For from man this one was taken!
> (Genesis 2:23, personal translation)

Stepping on Eggshells

The significance of this passage is difficult to state with sufficient care in this age of bruised feelings and quick tempers—on all sides. But this is an honest attempt to express what I believe to be the exquisite balance of Scripture.

Genesis 2:18-23 gives balance to the teaching of Genesis 1:26-28 concerning man as male and female. We have already asserted strongly and sincerely that man as male and female together reflects the image of God. There can be no biblical argument for inequality of persons based on gender. This statement remains true even though many have assumed inequality between the sexes and have acted in manifestly sinful ways.

But even among equals there may still be a relationship of priority. By the fact that Adam preceded his wife and gave her her name, we see his lordship. But by virtue of the fact that his name for her was a reflection of himself, we see their equality. Nahmanides paraphrased, "She is worthy of being called by the same name as myself."[15] We may say, "She at last, of all Yahweh's creatures, is also man in God's image." Or better, "The two of us together bear God's image as regents over his creation."

Theologians will continue to debate the concept of the image of God. Some attempt, erroneously in my estimation, to split bone and marrow in distinguishing "likeness" from "image" in Genesis 1:26. Some see the divine image solely in those moral and spiritual factors that distinguish man from beast. Others see the image of God reflected in the man-woman relationship as a mirror of the inner-relatedness of the Persons of the Trinity. Still others emphasize the rulership God delegated to man as the essential element of the divine image in man. In each of these suggestions there is one commonality: It is in the image of God that man has his dignity.

Dimensions of Dignity

In all our discussion and debate over the image of God in man, certain factors must not be overlooked. As we conclude this discussion of man in the image of God, let's look at some of those significant factors that should be kept in mind.

1. That man (and by extension woman) was made from the dust of the ground (Genesis 2:7) demonstrates his continuity with the physical world. The words of the curse emphasize this continuity: "for dust you are/ and to dust you will return" (Genesis 3:19).

2. That man was given an extended exposure to animal life in all its varied forms (Genesis 2:19-20) presented to him the anatomic similarities between himself and other creatures. It is not unbiblical, as some of my friends have insisted, for Christians to study comparative anatomy. This was one of the first tasks given to our parent.

3. That man, newly formed, was "inbreathed" by Yahweh and thereby became a living creature (Genesis 2:7) speaks of a special divine action that does not seem to allow for direct, organic continuity with prior creatures. If one wishes to speak of pre-Adamite humanoids (and we must not ignore the fossil record or dismiss it entirely as one grand humanist hoax—not every bone and skull was a Piltdown put-on!), one still has to reckon with the inbreathing of God that made Adam a living being.

> "The inbreathing was not an action superimposed upon an already animate being. . . . Man did not appear in two stages of animate development, and we may not think of man as possessing an animate life common to him and other beings, and then in addition an animate life distinct from other beings. The animation that is his is the animation that belongs to his distinguishing identity."[16]

4. That man was made in the image of God (Genesis 1:27) "is his differentia; it is his definition."[17] This concept of the image of God marks man out from his earthen frame as well as from his taxonomic partners. The image of God describes man in his whole being (including his body), in his relationship as male and female, in his potential for relationship with God his creator, and in his role as regent of Yahweh over the worlds God

has made. The image of God in man is inclusive and descriptive of his entire being. It is the essence of what man is.

5. The image of God described in Psalm 8, as we saw in the previous chapter, is worded with even more striking effect. Man was made to lack but little of God. It is as the image-bearer of God that man as male and female has his distinct dignity. This dignity, as we shall see in the next chapter, was not lost, but is greatly imperiled "east of Eden."

6. Biblical humanism is based upon the revelation of the image of God in man. Biblical humanism makes much of the Incarnation of the eternal Son of God, for with the Incarnation, God takes on humanity which was patterned after his own glory. Here is genuine mystery. All creation attests the wonder that man was made in God's image; now God himself, in the second member of the Trinity, has become an image-bearer!

"Where are you from?" I asked. Where indeed!

Chapter 6, Notes

1. Gerhard von Rad, *God at Work in Israel*, trans. by John H. Marks (Nashville: Abingdon Press, 1980), 103.

2. Ibid.

3. U. Cassuto, *A Commentary on the Book of Genesis, Part I: From Adam to Noah*, trans. by Israel Abrahams (Jerusalem: The Magnes Press, The Hebrew University, 1961), 57.

4. Robert L. Reymond, for example, bases his understanding of creation out of nothing in Genesis 1:1-3 on this word. He states, "the presence of *bara* makes it clear that the chapter is not concerned merely with the transformation of already existing material." (See Robert L. Reymond, "Does Genesis 1:1-3 Teach a Creation Out of Nothing?", *Creation Research Society Quarterly* 4 (1967):79.) In the same issue, John C. Whitcomb, Jr., suggests that since the verb *'aśah* is used in Genesis 1 as a synonym for *bara'*, it too must convey the idea of *creatio ex nihilo* ("The Creation of the Heavens and the Earth," 71).

5. A recent call for evangelicals to learn to appreciate the values of varied traditions in their worship is presented by Robert Schaper, *In His Presence: Appreciating Your Worship Tradition* (Nashville: Thomas Nelson, 1984). Gordon Borror and I have appealed for the reinstitution of creeds into "free church" worship in our book, *Worship: Rediscovering the Missing Jewel* (Portland, Ore.: Multnomah Press, 1982), 146-48. Characteristically, Robert E. Webber makes more than an appeal along this line; "Worship: A Methodology for Evangelical Renewal," *TSF Bulletin* 7 (Sept.-Oct., 1983):8-10.

6. Dietrich Bonhoeffer, *Creation and Fall: A Theological Interpretation of Genesis 1-3* (originally published in German in 1937; New York: Macmillan, 1959), 36.

7. This is an art form which the poets of the Bible learned from their cultural environment. A great many of the same devices found in the poetry of the Bible have their antecedents in the poetry of ancient Canaan as demonstrated by the poetic texts from Ugarit. I have developed the concept of parallelism in Hebrew poetry in my book, *Praise! A Matter of Life and Breath* (Nashville: Thomas Nelson, 1980), 41-56.

8. The terms translated "male" and "female" are explicitly sexual in denotation, referring to the respective reproductive organs, "the piercer" and "the pierced." Moreover, the wording of the verse decisively destroys the early rabbinic foolishness that originally man was a hermaphrodite. Our text says, "male and female he created *them*."

9. Paul K. Jewett, *Man as Male and Female: A Study in Sexual Relationships from a Theological Point of View* (Grand Rapids: Wm. B. Eerdmans Publishing Co., 1975), 20.

10. The KJV rendering "help meet" in Genesis 2:20 is an example of a good translation that is simply outdated and is consequently misunderstood as "helpmate." The archaic adjective "meet" was a fine translation of the Hebrew term which today may be translated "fitting" or "suitable."

11. Those who follow a tight six-day chronology for the creative week have to imagine the naming of the animals as taking place very rapidly toward the evening of the sixth day. For my part, I believe that this naming of the animals may well have stretched over a longer period of time.

12. James M. Houston, *I Believe in the Creator* (Grand Rapids: Wm. B. Eerdmans Publishing Co., 1980), 81.

13. Cassuto, *Genesis, Part I,* 130.

14. The words of Adam in Genesis 2:23 seem to demand this interpretation, but R. K. Harrison takes quite a different position, believing that the word "rib" means "an aspect of the personality." His view of this text is that of "religious drama." See his *Introduction to the Old Testament* (Grand Rapids: Wm. B. Eerdmans Publishing Co., 1969), 555-56.

15. Cassuto, *Genesis, Part I,* 136.

16. John Murray, *Collected Writings,* vol. 2, *Select Lectures in Systematic Theology* (Edinburgh: Banner of Truth, 1977), 8-9.

17. Ibid., 13.

Jews have another peculiarity that people comment on a lot. They always answer a question with a question. Well, why not? It reflects a special insight of our people, the knowledge that in this life there are no answers. All there are are questions. Two questions above all, and they are the same two that we ask always on this bus. Where have we come from?
Where are we going?
Judith Bruder
Going to Jerusalem

Chapter 7

East of Eden

*I*n her novel, *Going to Jerusalem,* Judith Bruder presents a contemporary update of an ancient masterpiece—and does so with a lovely twist. Her book is patterned after *The Canterbury Tales,* and the pilgrims are all American Jews (except for one Gentile). Along the way, amidst much humor, the reader learns something of the values of contemporary Judaism. One of the values is practicality—but practicality in paradox. The limitations of being human do not excuse one from living up to the divine image within.

> The rabbis saw that the only escape is between the horns of that dilemma into paradox. So Rabbi Tarfon says, It is not incumbent upon you to complete the task, yet you are not free to desist from it. To do the impossible while recognizing that it is impossible, that is what we are called upon to do.[1]

How Godlike Is God?

All of this makes for enjoyable reading. The question, however, is whether this presentation takes seriously either the blessed reality of the indescribable holiness of God or the terrible reality of the utter fallenness of man. There is paradox in true theology, but the paradox is not likely to be found in doing one's best to do the impossible and then relying on the kindness of God to cover the gap.

There is an attempt among some writers these days to exculpate God from the problem of evil in the world and to exaggerate the ability of man to live rightly in this world. God is viewed to have limited power to restrain evil or to have little interest in seeing evil held in check. As for man—he is to do his best, and that will be sufficient. What more could he be expected to do?

I am in agreement with Charles Colson in his repeated public criticism of Rabbi Harold S. Kushner's *When Bad Things Happen to Good People,* and in his even stronger criticism of evangelical leaders and pastors who have spoken well of that book. As Marguerite Shuster observes, Kushner gives no real theodicy because he does not play by the rules. Kushner explains the occurrences of evil in our lives as beyond the control of God by removing omnipotence from God. Meaning in evil is only subjective. "Most theists, however, will find such a God scarcely worthy of worship.² We cannot think rightly about either God or man unless we keep asking the questions Scripture demands—and seeking in the Scriptures for the answers.

What Has Happened?

Our study of Psalm 8 has led us to consider some of the most significant issues of life and faith. To the question, "What is man?" we have answered that man as male and female was made in the image of God to reflect his majesty upon the earth. If this is true, then we need to ask the question, "What has gone wrong?" There is simply too much nastiness, pettiness, and selfishness among the descendants of Adam for us to see majesty very often, in others or in ourselves.

We must move from man as God created him to man as he became—and now is. We cannot pretend that man is now as man was then when God pronounced his creation to be very good (Genesis 1:31). Even in Psalm 8 there is word of trouble in man. Verse 2 speaks of enemies of God, of the foe and the avenger. Even the Psalm that speaks of man's majesty speaks of his ignobility. To understand this, we need to go back to Eden— and follow man east.

Back to Eden

The story of the fall of man in Genesis 3 is presented in a childlike, yet never childish, way. That is, the account reads as a story told to children; but the content of the story is of such vast import that no child could be expected to understand it adequately. Nor are we likely to understand it, at least not fully. The narrative is childlike because of the presentation of innocence and its loss. The story is permeated with mystery, yet commands our attention because of our perception of its reality. C. Stephen Evans observes that the fall of man is one of the most difficult biblical doctrines to understand, yet the sinful nature of man is one of the most well-attested of Christian doctrines: "There is hardly any doctrine which seems to have such massive experiential support."[3]

The Snake in the Garden

You know the story. It is an account that begins with innocence and blessedness. In classical literary terms, the garden setting of the story is ideal.[4] In fact, our English word "paradise" is ultimately derived from the term "garden." I doubt that we can imagine a picture of paradise apart from a lush and peaceful garden scene.

The story ends in genuine tragedy, and the course is through temptation and the rite of initiation. Man as male and female moves from the closest relationship possible with God to an estrangement forced by an armed angel—such is the course of the narrative.

Eve and Adam and the Way East

What a moment it was in our history when Eve, our mother, reached out for the fruit which Yahweh had forbidden! At the outstretching of her hand, was there not the shrinking back of all creation? Milton captures the cosmic terror of the moment:

> So saying, her rash hand in evil hour
> Forth reaching to the fruit, she plucked, she eat:
> Earth felt the wound, and nature from her seat
> Sighing through all her works gave signs of woe,
> That all was lost.[5]

At that point, his evil work accomplished, the serpent slunk back as Eve ate the fruit:

> Greedily she engorged without restraint,
> And knew not eating death.[6]

Unlike Eve, who was deceived, Adam sinned with eyes wide open and by that sin—together with Eve—had his eyes opened in a new and terrible manner. On realizing his sin and his loss, the man turned on his mate as mutual blame flew back and forth:

> Is this the love, is this the recompense
> Of mine to thee, ingrateful Eve, expressed
> Immutable when thou wert lost, not I,
> Who might have lived and joyed immortal bliss,
> Yet willingly chose rather death with thee:
> And am I now upbraided, as the cause
> Of thy transgressing?[7]

All was lost, but all was lost together. And all was affected profoundly. Creation itself was stung, order was now inter-mixed with disorder, cosmos with chaos, flowers with thorns. Naked lovers searched for clothing, a new embarrassment in one another's presence compounded by a terror of the visit of dearest Friend. From the Friend came words of a Foe, yet new words of a Friend as well. And together, coping with disaster, decay, and death, our parents went east of the garden as an angel blocked their return.

Believing Too Little or Too Much

Just as it is possible to err by believing either too little or too much in the existence and power of demons, so it is possible to err by either denying or exaggerating the reality and consequences of the Fall. Exaggerating the consequences of the Fall takes some doing, however, for they are so truly disastrous that we shall never fully comprehend them.

For nontheistic humanists as well as for liberal religionists, the fall of man is hardly taken seriously.

> The religious description of man as "corrupt" is always an impassable stumbling block for humanism, whatever its variety. When humanists speak of man's corruption, inhumanity, and demonic qualities, they do *not* mean thereby to give a complete and final description.[8]

Occasionally one encounters a secular writer who describes "demonic qualities" in man, but this seems to be done for literary effect. Rarely are such descriptions based on biblical theology. William L. Shirer, for example, introduces Adolf Hitler as having "a demonic personality, a granite will, uncanny instincts, a cold ruthlessness, a remarkable intellect, a soaring imagination and—until toward the end, when drunk with power and success, he overreached himself—an amazing capacity to size up people and situations."[9] The description of the archvillain of modern history as "demonic" would be fitting in the judgment of most readers. Few would think of themselves as equally subject to demonic influence or having a similarly fallen nature.

Comfort for the Dead

For most people in our day, man is viewed as sick—but not dead. Man is believed to be weak—but not dead. Man is said to be diseased—but not dead. Modern man does not take seriously the teaching of the Fall; modern churchmen seem not to take it seriously either. Many religionists who ought to know better urge positive theology, not the dark and depressing realities of the effects of the primeval fall of man. Some even speak of a new reformation based on self-esteem as the greatest need for our day.

But if we take the Fall seriously, we need to ask some questions. We need to ask how a dead man might think positively about himself. How can a person who is dead develop a sense of self-esteem that will affect morbidity? If one is really dead, then these are phantom thoughts. They are self-deceiving and a misuse of language.

Despite the terrible possibilities of nuclear devastation in our age, many people prefer to be romantics, seeking a Camelot that never was and denying the possibility of nuclear war. Too often churchmen follow in this same practice. The possibility of humans destroying the world by the unleashing of the frightful weapons available today is still only statistical; it is not certain. But the fact of the coming judgment of Yahweh on the wicked men of this earth is not just a statistical probability. It is as sure as his existence, for this bitter reality is tied to his very character (2 Peter 3:8-13).

Speaking of self-esteem as man's greatest need is akin to an observer at a funeral parlor remarking, "How wonderfully lifelike!" as he views the corpse. We need to face the issue squarely: Dead people need life, not make-up; fallen people need redemption, not self-esteem. Jesus did not come to earth to make dead people feel better about themselves. He came to dead men to give them life (Luke 19:10; John 10:10).

Man in Revolt

What was the Fall, then? It was more than a stain or a blemish. The fall of man in our first parents was a complete and utter revolt against the person of God as revealed by his sovereignty, supremacy, authority, and will. John Murray says that the Fall was "an assault upon the divine Majesty, repudiation of his sovereignty and authority, doubt of his goodness, dispute with his wisdom, [and a] contradiction of his veracity."[10]

We simply cannot come to a biblical understanding of man nor to a biblical appreciation of salvation if we do not come to grips with the awfulness of man in rebellion, separation, and death. We are profoundly fallen. Man's arrogant desire for autonomy from God, which was an act of rebellion against the Creator's authority and benevolence, has caused havoc. The curse that resulted "affected not only man's spiritual relationship with God and his personal and social relationships, but also his whole economic and material environment."[11]

"In Adam's Fall We Sinned All"

Once we have a biblical view of the ghastly results of the Fall of man, it is difficult to underestimate its effects. *McGuffey's Readers* had it right all along. Man and his environment, his relationships and his own being—all were affected by the sin of our parents. The extent of the effects of the Fall are universal. The fall of man was our own fall. We were there in Adam, and we stand there on our own accord in our own experience. The majesty of man is often hard to find east of Eden. As David was to write thousands of years after the Fall, with history already full of the evil actions of man:

> All have turned aside,
>   they have together become corrupt;
> there is no one who does good,
>   not even one.
>
>   (Psalm 14:3)

David did not come to this dour conclusion because of personal pique. He received it from Yahweh by means of revelation. In the pictorial language of Psalm 14, David speaks of Yahweh looking down from heaven in divine incredulity searching for one individual who was not like milk that had soured. But the totality were in apostasy. The corruption is universal. You and I, dear reader, are not excepted.[12]

A millennium later the apostle Paul came to the same conclusion and reasserted the words of David (Romans 3:9-12). Such a result cannot be trivialized. Yet the Fall continues to astound us: How could it have happened?

Mystery and Intentionality

There is a great deal of mystery in the story of the Fall. We are told nothing about the origin of evil in the serpent. We are informed only that the serpent was extraordinarily crafty; albeit a creature of God, he perverted the word of God and seduced the woman into her act of betrayal. The Bible leaves the origin of evil in the serpent a mystery, a riddle. The Bible mocks us in our curiosity to know the source of evil in the serpent. Nothing in the first two chapters of Genesis has prepared us for it. All of God's creation was declared by the Creator to be good. We simply cannot come to terms with the origin of evil; it is inexplicable from this text.

This is as it should be. For it is not the intention of Scripture to explain to us how evil entered the cosmos of the Creator. Scripture tells us how evil entered the life of man. It is not that there is no answer; it is that the answer of the origin of evil in the universe is not necessary to explain the rise of evil in man. The evil of the serpent may not be used to dismiss the evil act in man. The fall of man demonstrates that "there always has been, there always will be defection. . . . Man is such that under certain circumstances he can be seduced."[13] And the blame for his seduction cannot be transferred to the tempter. The temptation was the occasion, the provocation; the sin was a deliberate act on the part of our parents—an act they were free not to do. Once the act was done, however, they remained no longer free not to sin. Man is now free only to increase his rebellion.[14]

The Fall and the Image

Given the terrible reality of the fall of man and its consequences, how is it possible to exaggerate its results? It scarcely seems possible for the results of the Fall to be fully realized by us, much less to be overstated. But we are in danger of overstating the results of the Fall if we judge that man after the Fall is no longer a creature of dignity bearing the image of God.

The genuine paradox of theology is not that man must try to do that which he cannot do, and then allow God to fill the gap (as in some popular misconceptions we have already noted).

The stunning paradox of biblical theology is that even in his rebellion man bears God's image.

Some feel that to argue in this way is to reduce or minimize
the consequences of the Fall. As a matter of fact, it is in arguing
this way that we remain not only biblical (and hence realistic),
but we maximize the consequences of the Fall. For if those who
are fallen still bear God's image, then their condition is wors-
ened. When fallen people sin, and in their sin they still bear
God's image, then their sin is all the more heinous.

Long after sin had entered the heart of man and irreparably
marred his being, he still bore the likeness of God (Genesis 5:1-
2). Moreover, that image of God was transmitted to his offspring, along with death and depravity. The litany of Genesis 5,
"and then he died," occurs together with the affirmation of
man's identity as an image bearer of God (5:1-2). Similarly, the
fact that man bears the image of God is the reason given for the
institution of capital punishment. The person who destroys
another person made in God's image will justly have his own
life taken (Genesis 9:6).

Shame Man—Shame God

Lest one think that is "only Old Testament teaching"
(gasp!), we point to James 3:9:

> With the tongue we praise our Lord and Father, and
> with it we curse men, who have been made in God's
> likeness.

This verse demonstrates a wry insight into human personality.
James has just observed that the dominion God expected man to
manifest over the animal life has largely been accomplished:
"All kinds of animals, birds, reptiles and creatures of the sea are
being tamed and have been tamed by man" (3:7). But the one
creature that man has yet to tame is his own tongue: "But no man
can tame the tongue. It is a restless evil, full of deadly poison"
(v. 8). In this misuse of the tongue we find that our folly in cursing an individual is in fact an attack that ultimately brings shame
on God. When a man, in whose being the image of God rests, is

cursed, the image of God within him is contemned. Is this not a possible reason for our Lord's words concerning the misuse of the tongue in anger against another (Matthew 5:21-22)?

James is speaking of fallen man and sinful actions. But fallen and sinful men still bear the image of God and are to be treated with dignity.

Worth and Dignity

We are not here speaking of man as worthy of salvation. He is not. Man is not at all worthy of God's grace. Salvation is God's surprise to those who are most *un*worthy. But man still has dignity—even under the curse of sin and death. For man, fallen man, still bears the mark of his Maker.

Imagine coming across an abused Stradivarius violin. I have in mind not just a violin with a broken bridge, but one whose neck is broken and belly damaged, with ribs destroyed and fingerboard gone. Now one person might think of this badly damaged instrument as a piece of junk and hardly give it notice. But another might look more closely and find the name of the master Antonio Stradivari still legible on the broken instrument and recognize the worth of the damaged goods. At once his heart is broken that such an instrument could have been so abused; at the same time he makes plans to restore the instrument even if he must mortgage his home to do so. He will take that broken instrument to the finest violin maker available and ask that it be restored lovingly and faithfully to the best possible approximation of its original beauty.

So it is with man. It is a mistake to regard even the most damaged of men as worthless. For despite the most awful of flaws and grievous of sins, there is still on this wretch the mark of the Master Yahweh. When we sense how terrible it is that one bearing God's image is fallen, we cannot but mourn. But we also long for a faithful restoration, knowing that in this case the restoration can be accomplished only by the original Maker himself.

Man is thus a mystery. He has within himself, as Pascal observed, greatness and misery.

As it strikes us, this phrase is in our day often quoted to emphasize that man's "greatness" has revealed itself in astonishing ways in this century and, on the other hand, man's misery and evil, his destructive capacities, have become just as obvious. A variety of views about man, the secret of his nature, his mysterious and riddle-filled nature, often circle around these two words—greatness and misery. Precisely this alienating contrast has been referred to as man's "unique paradoxicality."[15]

Man is fallen but man has dignity. Though he is unable to right himself with deity, he still bears his Maker's mark. Whereas man was once free to worship God and to serve him in integrity, now man is free only to increase his rebellion and worsen his standing. Only a doctrine of radical depravity will do justice to the nonchildish account of man's fall. Only a doctrine of magnificent dignity will be in accord with the teaching of man's creation.

Here is the genuine paradox; here is the unsolvable riddle. The awfulness of fallenness is balanced by the awesomeness of image-bearing. The great depth of sin is matched by the great worth of man. These antinomies serve as God's justification for the earth-and-heaven troubling that led to the Incarnation.

There is a gulf between man and God that none but God may bridge. And even he could bridge it only by means of himself. God bridged that gulf because of what he treasured in man—his own image. Man who is not worthy does have some worth.

Even fallen man? That is the only kind of man there is, save God who became Man in Christ! And in Christ man may regain what it truly means to be fully human.

Evangelicals are pessimistic with regard to what human beings can do on their own but optimistic about what God can accomplish in and through them. Grace does not reduce man to nothingness but instead raises him to fellowship with his Creator.

Irenaeus put it succinctly: "The glory of God is man fully alive." Amandus Polanus, sixteenth-century Basel professor and Reformer, stated the complementary truth: "The glory of man is the living God."[16]

It is precisely because of the high value that Yahweh places in man—who, though fallen, still bears his image—that God himself became man in Christ.

Chapter 7, Notes

1. Judith Bruder, *Going to Jerusalem* (New York: Simon and Schuster, 1979), 310.

2. Marguerite Shuster, "The Good, the Bad and The Troubled: Studies in Theodicy," *TSF Bulletin* (Sept.-Oct., 1983), 7. Kushner's book was published in New York by Schocken, 1981. Colson's criticism has been given in many public and written forms; he made this forcefully in his address for the commencement of Western Conservative Baptist Seminary, June 1983. See Dave Bourne, "Living the Faith," *Christian Life*, January 1984, 70-71.

3. C. Stephen Evans, *Preserving the Person: A Look at the Human Sciences* (Grand Rapids: Baker Book House, 1982), 146.

4. Leland Ryken has a fine development of the literary elements in the story of Paradise and Fall. See his *The Literature of the Bible* (Grand Rapids: Zondervan Publishing House, 1974), 37-42.

5. John Milton, *Paradise Lost and Other Poems*, ed. Maurice Kelley (Roslyn, N.Y.: Walter J. Black, 1943), Book IX, 301.

6. Ibid.

7. Ibid., 311-12.

8. G. C. Berkouwer, *Man: The Image of God (Studies in Dogmatics)*, trans. Dirk W. Jellema (Grand Rapids: Wm. B. Eerdmans Publishing Co., 1962), 17.

9. William L. Shirer, *The Rise and Fall of the Third Reich: A History of Nazi Germany* (New York: Simon and Schuster, 1960), 6.

10. John Murray, *Collected Writings*, vol. 2: *Select Lectures in Systematic Theology* (London: Banner of Truth Trust, 1977), 70.

11. Christopher J. H. Wright, *An Eye for an Eye: The Place of Old Testament Ethics Today* (Downers Grove, Ill.: InterVarsity Press, 1983), 71.

12. I have developed the message of Psalm 14 in my book on the prophetic Psalms. See Ronald Barclay Allen, *When Song Is New: Understanding the Kingdom in the Psalms* (Nashville: Thomas Nelson, 1983), 129-49.

13. Claus Westermann, *Creation*, trans. John Scullion (Philadelphia: Fortress Press, 1974), 92.

14. This point is made more fully by James Montgomery Boice, *God the Redeemer*, vol. 2, *Foundations of the Christian Faith* (Downers Grove, Ill.: InterVarsity Press, 1979), 43-48.

15. Berkouwer, *Man*, 16. The expression "unique paradoxicality" is from K. H. A. Hidding.

16. Donald G. Bloesch, *The Future of Evangelical Christianity* (Garden City, N.Y.: Doubleday, 1983), 19-20.

I see myself at the Last Judgment, and, as at an earthly trial, my identity has to be established before the proceedings begin. But there is an interruption. The Supreme Judge has hardly put to me the question, "Who are you?" before my satanic accuser breaks in and answers for me, "Who is he, you ask? I will tell you. He is the one who has done such and such, and failed to do such and such. He has ignored the plight of his neighbors because he himself was always the neighbor. He has been silent when he ought to have confessed. The gifts you have given him have not made him humble but proud." He goes on for a long time in this strain. But then the counsel for the defense interrupts; he is the exalted Son of God. "O Father and Judge," he says, "the prosecutor has spoken the truth. This man has all these things behind him. But the accusation is without substance. For he no longer is what he has behind him." And although he who sits on the bench knows very well what Christ is saying, for the sake of the audience he asks, "Who is he then if he is no longer what he has behind him?" To this Christ replies, "He has become my disciple and believed me that you have met him in me and want to be his father, as you are mine. Hence I have canceled his past and nailed the accusation to my cross [Colossians 2:14]. Who is he then, you ask? He is the one who has accepted me and thus gained the right of sonship that you have promised. Look upon him, then, as you look upon me; he is my brother and your son." This is the story of our identity.

Helmut Thielicke
Being Human . . . Becoming Human

Chapter 8

Man in Christ

*T*he question, "What is Man?" simply will not go away. Whenever we question our identity or the meaning of our existence, we keep coming back to this fundamental question. The more troubled our day becomes, the more haunting the question. "We ask about ourselves only when we are insecure, when our identity has ceased to be self-evident and, unquestionably, when we see ourselves exposed."[1] As Adam, we are now quite conscious of our own nakedness in this age of nuclear madness, technological manipulation, and the general depersonalization of society.

The answers to the question of meaning seem to be as varied as the number of people who respond. It is likely, however, that we shall never come to a sound answer to the meaning of man until we learn to assert rightly the humanity of the Savior. Until we come to a genuine appreciation of the humanity of the Lord Jesus Christ, we shall not be able to come to grips with our own. Our humanity is now enwrapped in his. A deficient view of the humanity of the Lord will lead us to think, along with far too many others, that being human is merely a matter of breath or dust or beastliness.

Man but Breath

There is a sense in which man is but a passing breath. This is not just an idea of disillusioned man; it is an assertion found in the Bible itself.

Stop trusting in man,
who has but a breath in his nostrils.
Of what account is he? (Isaiah 2:22).

Life is fleeting. Like grass on a thatched roof, man is here today but is gone in a moment's blast of hot desert wind (Isaiah 37:27). If it is the breath of God that has given man life (Genesis 2:7), it is the breath of God that can take it away:

All men are like grass,
and all their glory is like the flowers of the field.
The grass withers and the flowers fall,
because the breath of the LORD blows on them.
Surely the people are grass (Isaiah 40:6-7).

Dust to Dust

Not only is life fleeting and man frail, but we also often wonder, "What is the point of it all?" A rich man dies, a poor man dies—in a hundred years what difference is there in the relative value of their caskets? Do the worms care? Man was made from the dust and man returns to the dust—his very name is dust![2] As the old joke has it, if man is from dust and going to dust, "Mommy, someone is either coming or going under the bed." If man is dust, then "What's the point?"

"Meaningless! Meaningless!"
says the Teacher.
"Utterly meaningless!
Everything is meaningless" (Ecclesiastes 1:2).

Man and Beast

Another aspect of man is creatureliness. Man is created, not creator; man is dependent, not independent; man is akin to the great ape as well as to the lizard and the hummingbird. Like them he is dependent upon a complex spectrum of factors for his existence. Within a narrow range of toleration he lives and thrives; outside that narrow range he perishes like a goldfish outside the bowl. Like the beasts, he is dependent—constantly dependent—for the very breath he breathes.

But man also possesses a dignity that far surpasses that of the animals. It is to God that man is drawn, not to the animals. It is with Yahweh that man converses, not with animals. Man is so distinct from the animals that there is an impassible barrier between them despite their family relationship as fellow-creatures of the sixth day. It is because of this distance that the Scriptures are so severe in their condemnation of any sexual relationship between man and beast (Exodus 22:19; Leviticus 18:23; 20:15-16).[3] Not only is this a grievous evil, man in covenant with God is to say "Amen!" to God's condemnation of such behavior (Deuteronomy 27:21).

Man and Dignity

Man is nearer to God than any of God's creatures. His differentia—that which makes him what he is—is that he is made in the divine image. "Alongside the statement of man's ephemeral and limited nature the Old Testament proclaims unceasingly the eminent dignity conferred upon him by his peculiar associations with God."[4]

Man in the image of God is a majestic creature; he has great dignity in the eyes of his Maker. Even fallen man continues to bear the image of God. It is that fact that deepens the disaster of man's fallenness, and it is that fact that makes the concept of eternal perdition so truly awful. The eternal damnation of an image-bearer of God is an unspeakable horror. It is not just that a wicked man is lost forever; it is rather that a man made in God's image is lost forever. If an obscenity is a degrading misuse of a term or concept of honor, the lostness of man in God's image is the ultimate obscenity.

Man's Alien Dignity

Now here is the wonder. When a person comes to a saving knowledge of the Lord Jesus Christ, he not only has life forever, but he is now more man than ever. Christ restores what it truly means to be human. In Christ we are given a new aspect of our history with God and participate in a new way in what Thielicke, following Luther, calls the "alien dignity" of man.[5]

Our beginning as a *race* was in bestowed dignity; we were made in the divine image (Genesis 1:26-28). Our beginning as *persons* is also in bestowed dignity; our Maker is involved with us from the moment of conception through the entire process of fetal formation:

> For you created my inmost being;
>> you knit me together in my mother's womb.
> I praise you because I am fearfully and
>> wonderfully made;
>> your works are wonderful,
>> I know that full well.
> My frame was not hidden from you
>> when I was made in the secret place.
> When I was woven together in the depths of the earth,
>> your eyes saw my unformed body.
>>>> (Psalm 139:13-16a)[6]

We have been made in God's image, crafted from conception by his marvelous care and wisdom. But our *new beginning* is found in our relationship with Christ, the new Adam who is truly God and truly man. Only God could have brought about our new beginning, and God could do this only as he became man in Christ. Here is the great mystery of our faith and its true definition. The impact of a sound view of the Person of the Lord Jesus Christ on our own sense of humanity ought to be enormous.

The Seed of Heresy

The doctrine of the Person of Christ is one of the most difficult, and one of the most important, of all biblical issues to state correctly. In the early centuries of the church it was the precise definition of the doctrine of Christ that occupied the great minds and provoked the sharpest controversies. Deviations from the biblical view of the nature of the Person of Christ came early and strong. Balance in Christology was precarious nearly from the beginning.

In his new book on heresy and credal formation,[7] Harold O. J. Brown traces from the earliest period to our own day the debates concerning the nature of Christ. He shows that there is something far worse for thoughtful Christians than paganism in the world about us. That which is worse is the perversion of truth from within the community of faith. Heresy comes from within, not from without. An atheist is an outsider to faith and has no claim to the term "heresy." Only one within the camp may earn the description heretic, but the earning of this description is no prize.

There is no truth more subject to perversion (and no perversion more heinous) than the doctrine of the Person of the Savior. Go wrong here, and one goes wrong everywhere. Here is the domino theory of theology.

The Faith of the Fathers

The church did not come easily to a definitive statement on the nature of the Person of Christ.

> Between the death and resurrection of Christ and the Council of Chalcedon in 451, over four centuries had passed. It took four centuries for most Christians to arrive at a statement (not an explanation) of the relationship between God and man in Jesus Christ.[8]

It was at Chalcedon that the theologians of the church were finally able to state the correct biblical balance of the doctrine of Christ. This statement includes the following principal ideas:

- Jesus Christ is true God.
- Jesus Christ is true man.
- Jesus Christ is One Person.
- Jesus Christ has two natures.

The Errors of Their Sons

The history of Christological heresy is a history of the distortion or misstatement of these basic ideas. Some have so emphasized the deity of Jesus that they have lost sight of his humanity. Others have so emphasized the humanity of Jesus that they have lost sight of his deity.

The errors have abounded through time. Some have denied that Christ has two natures; others have confused his one Person with his two natures. Another early heresy claimed that Jesus was a man who was adopted into the Godhead as the Holy Spirit came upon him in his baptism—a view that one still hears today from time to time. Many have had fuzzy thoughts about the innerworkings of the Trinity and have viewed the members of the Trinity in a modalistic form: God appears in the mode of Father or the mode of Son or Spirit as his work demands, but he is not truly three Persons in unity.

Vinegar in Wine Skins

Some evangelicals are quite careless about the doctrine of Christ and the Trinity. It is shocking that some seem to feel these issues do not matter much any more. Serious and pressing discussions in this area are viewed by some as divisive and disruptive to Christian harmony. The fact that earlier Christians were willing to die for these issues—and indeed did die for them— seems hardly to matter today.

A couple of years ago I had a most disagreeable interchange with an adult Sunday school teacher who ministers in a Bible-teaching church. He is an outstanding teacher who works hard to prepare his lessons and communicates them well. The problem is that he forthrightly denies the doctrine of the Trinity. Because I was suspicious that this might be the case, I came prepared to the interchange with a copy of the Nicene Creed[9] which I read to him and asked him to comment on. He clearly denied that the creed was biblical, true, or his own viewpoint. It is my understanding that he still teaches an adult class in his orthodox church; further confrontation of his false doctrine presumably is regarded as "divisive." If we shrink today from the brutal killing of heretics done by our forefathers, have we correspondingly lost all concern for heresy among the teachers in our own churches? The wine skins now hold vinegar; few care to take the time to smell or tell.

God—Yes; Man—?

We must learn to think rightly about the Person of Christ and the Trinity. These are the issues of the faith. They may not be minimized. Generally we do fairly well when we consider the deity of the Savior, but less well when we think of his humanity.

When we think of witnessing to others about our Christian faith, do we not tend to give much attention to arguments for the deity of the Son of God? We likely feel that this issue is so important that we cannot be unprepared. We likewise go to great pains to stress the deity of the Savior in home Bible classes, clinics on witnessing, and Sunday school classes for all ages. Yet we do not emphasize as strongly his own words that he is the Son of Man. Rarely do we get exercised over his humanity. I suspect that the hardest issue for many Christians to accept is that Jesus Christ was truly man. We tend to argue strongly for his deity, but simply to assume his humanity. Such strains of doceticism may still be heard in the preaching of the church, but are more likely to be found in the folkways of Christian people.

In early Christianity there was an equally strong tendency to emphasize the true deity of the Savior, but deny or minimize his true humanity.

> The claims the New Testament makes for Jesus Christ, and the impression he made on his followers, were so overwhelming that it was very difficult to conceive of him as really ever having been a man. The early Christians found it easier to accept Christ as God than to admit that, being God, he was also truly man. Marcion, the gnostics, and others as well resolved this problem simply by flatly denying that Jesus was truly human. Orthodoxy will ultimately strongly affirm his full humanity in credal

statements, but even the orthodox will be troubled by
a recurring tendency to see him as only divine, to the
neglect of his humanity.[10]

So long as Christians have difficulty giving assent to the
genuine humanity of the Savior, Christians are likely to have
difficulty coming to terms with their own humanity.

The Spirit of Antichrist

Yet the New Testament seems to have anticipated this deficient view of the Savior. John, the very apostle who presents
so much convincing data concerning the deity of the Lord Jesus
Christ, is the one who fights so strongly any denial of the humanity of Jesus of Nazareth. He recounts that Jesus was no mere
appearance, but was true man perceived by the normal senses of
his fellows (1 John 1:1-3). What are the marks of antichrist?
They are to deny that Jesus is the Messiah (1 John 2:22-23), or to
deny that Jesus came *in the flesh* (1 John 4:2-3). Already in
John's day there were false teachers who denied that Jesus
Christ had come in the flesh (2 John 7); such are deceivers and
they are to be rejected, lest one join in their wickedness (vv. 10-
11).

Sound theology demands a balanced view of the Person of
the Savior Jesus. It is unfortunate that contemporary biblical
teaching is not stronger in this area, for we must learn to think
rightly about the One who is God and man. To learn to think
rightly about his humanity is to rediscover the meaning of our
own humanity created in the image of God.

The Word Became Flesh

Think again of the wonder-words of John 1:14,

> The Word became flesh and lived for a while among
> us. We have seen his glory, the glory of the one and
> only Son, who came from the Father, full of grace
> and truth.

In these words we have the center of history, the Grand
Miracle, the basis of our redemption—*God became man.* He

who existed before there was a cosmos has become flesh and has entered, in space and time, the cosmos which he made. *God became man*. Who the Word was is made clear from John 1:1. *God*—that is what he was! But *man*—that is what he became!

I doubt that any of us can really grasp what it meant for God to become man. There is still room in theology for the term "mystery." Certainly the Incarnation is a genuine mystery of the faith, but it is essential to all thinking that is Christian.

Our difficulty in giving adequate expression to the mystery of the Incarnation shows at once the enormity of the issue. We have difficulty stating the matter clearly, without lapsing into one of many errors. We must affirm again the essential truths concerning the Person of Christ: he is true God, he is true man, he is One Person, he has two natures.

We learn as children that God became man in the birth of Jesus at Bethlehem. Perhaps it is only as children that we can state this wonder simply and truly.

Gospel and Old Testament

It is remarkable to me that the God-Man relationship in Jesus Christ was anticipated in the Old Testament before it was ever accomplished in the records of the New Testament. The Hebrew Scriptures speak with remarkable clarity and specificity concerning the Person of the Savior. This is done in type as well as in explicit text.

We often read Micah 5:2 during Advent and emphasize the prophecy of the place where the Savior was to be born. It is not a little matter to observe that the eighth-century prophet Micah prophesied the very city of the birth of Jesus. But Micah also speaks of the nature of the one to be born with delicate balance and insight. Read these words with that issue in mind:

> "But you, Bethlehem Ephrathah,
>   though you are small among the clans of Judah,
> out of you will come for me
>   one who will be ruler over Israel,
> whose origins are from of old,
>   from ancient times."

The baby who was to be born in Bethlehem is the eternal One. As Jesus said to his incredulous antagonists, "before Abraham was born, I am!" (John 8:58). His audacious claim was that he was the eternal One, Yahweh of Sinai, very God— and yet very man. And Micah saw something of this seven centuries before the fact.

Isaiah, the noble contemporary of the rural Micah, saw it as well and expressed the marvel more fully, but no more sensitively:

> For to us a child is born,
> > to us a son is given,
> > and the government will be on his shoulders.
> And he will be called
> > Wonderful Counselor, Mighty God,
> > Everlasting Father, Prince of Peace (Isaiah 9:6).

In this verse of exquisite and delicate balance, there is the supreme presentation of the deity and the humanity of the Savior Jesus, presented seven centuries before he actually became flesh.

- As God he is—a son who is given;
- As Man he is—a child who is born.

When God Was Born as Man

Christmas pageants remind us that Jesus was born as a baby, but few look on the manger and really think BABY. We teach our children to sing the sentimental words, "no crying he makes." If Jesus was a baby, we imagine that he must have been a prodigy indeed, blessing shepherds and little drummer boys alike from his manger.

Yet baby he was—a baby in every sense of that word. Jesus did not bless the shepherds; he nursed at his mother's breast. Jesus did not speak to the cattle or cushion his manger or mend Joseph's garment. As all older siblings observe about their little baby brothers or sisters, he slept . . . he wept . . . he nursed . . . he went . . . and he slept again.

He is the one whose goings forth have been from everlasting, but he was also a human baby born in the normal manner, needing the care of his blessed mother. He created the universe; but helpless, he needed a diaper change. He placed the stars and stretched the expanse, but was now subject to colds and colic, to rash and runny nose. The omnipotent God became vulnerable; the eternal One had a new beginning. There is no mystery in all the universe to be compared with the mystery of the Incarnation.

Son of Adam, Son of God

For these reasons the Lord Jesus Christ may be called the son of Adam, as he is in the magnificent genealogy of Luke 3. Luke carefully begins by saying that Jesus "was the son, so it was thought, of Joseph"—a wry reference to his virgin birth (Luke 3:23). But Luke concludes his litany of names in this way: "the son of Enos, the son of Seth, the son of Adam, the son of God" (Luke 3:38). Here the human line of Jesus is traced back to Adam who was the son of God by immediate creation. There could be no more weighty a presentation of the humanity of the Savior.

Son of God—Uniquely

But he is not only "the son of Adam, the son of God"; Jesus is the unique Son of God in his own right, with no intermediary (John 1:14). Jesus the son of Adam, the son of God, is also the Son of God who was ever at the Father's side (John 1:18). Whereas all who are redeemed may be called the children of God (John 1:12), only the Savior Jesus is the unique Son of God. He is the one and only.[11]

First Adam—Last Adam

Further, it is as man that Jesus Christ is the second Adam. The first Adam brought death in his life; the new Adam brings life through his death. It was through our father Adam that death came into the world (Romans 5:12); it is through our Father Jesus that eternal life is manifested once more (5:21). The connection between Adam and Jesus is so strong in Paul's mind that he is able to speak of Adam as "a pattern of the one to come" (5:14). He writes, "For as in Adam all die, so in Christ all will be made alive" (1 Corinthians 15:22), and again, "So it is written: 'The first man Adam became a living being'; the last Adam, a life-giving spirit" (15:45).

"Behold the Man"

That which Adam lost, Christ restored. Sin and death came from the first Adam; forgiveness and life from the last Adam. It was only in becoming man that Jesus could accomplish what man had lost. It was only as God that Jesus could become man. In anticipation of his work as man, the second member of the Trinity left heaven and entered the world with the words:

> "Sacrifice and offering you did not desire,
> but a body you prepared for me; . . .
> Then I said, 'Here I am—it is written about me
> in the scroll—
> I have come to do your will, O God.' "
>
> (Hebrews 10:5, 7)

Augustine spoke of Christ as "the one who, already Son of God, came to become Son of man, so as to give us who were already sons of men the power to become sons of God" (Letter 140).

Son of Man

As is well-known, a distinctive name the Lord Jesus used of himself was "Son of Man."

And it is the prophet Daniel who gives those words the unique meaning that makes them so appropriate for our Savior in his incarnation. Daniel, like Isaiah and John, had a vision of God in glory on his throne. In his stunning vision, Daniel saw God as "the Ancient of Days" seated on the throne that flamed with fire, surrounded by myriads of attendants. As Daniel kept watching that which man may not see, he saw one approach the seated Ancient of Days and an extraordinary transfer took place:

"In my vision at night I looked, and there before me
was one like a son of man, coming with the clouds of
heaven. He approached the Ancient of Days and was
led into his presence. He was given authority, glory
and sovereign power; all peoples, nations and men of
every language worshiped him. His dominion is an
everlasting dominion that will not pass away, and his
kingdom is one that will never be destroyed (Daniel
7:13-14).

Here the words "one like a son of man" refer to the Lord
Jesus, whom Daniel saw in supernal glory before the throne of
the Father, the Ancient of Days. The context of royalty is not
without importance for our discussion.

Man is majestic—or so God made him. When God made
man as male and female he crowned him with glory and honor
and gave to him power and dominion over all that God had
made. When Adam and Eve rebelled against God, in some
measure they lost the prerogative of rule; to some extent they
lost their royal mantle. But to another Man these prerogatives
are given. These powers and authorities are given to "one like a
son of man" in the vision of Daniel. They are given to the one
who became the Son of Man in flesh in the Incarnation of Jesus.

From Where One Stands

Our standpoint causes us to be amazed that the Bible presents a Man as truly God. From the standpoint of the Incarnate
One, the real marvel is that eternal God could become Man. Is
this not the likely reason for the Lord's regular designation of
himself as "the Son of Man"? When Jesus uses this phrase he
may emphasize the incongruity of his humanity, as when he
compares himself to animals in terms of creature comfort and
the holding of possessions:

"Foxes have holes and birds of the air have nests, but
the Son of Man has no place to lay his head"
(Matthew 8:20).

All Man Was Meant to Be

The Savior may also use this phrase to assert his royal authority and essential deity:

> "But so that you may know that the Son of Man has authority on earth to forgive sins. . . ." Then he said to the paralytic, "Get up, take your mat and go home." And the man got up and went home. When the crowd saw this, they were filled with awe; and they praised God, who had given such authority to men (Matthew 9:6-8).

In this text we see the royal nature of the phrase, "the Son of Man," which we might have anticipated from Daniel's vision. By this designation Jesus asserted that his identification with humanity was complete. But by this designation he also asserted that his identification with humanity was with humanity as it ought to be: royal, wonderful, majestic. And how the crowd marveled—here was the authority of God being demonstrated by a Man. Might their thoughts have gone back to Genesis 1 or Psalm 8? Our thoughts must make that connection. The new Adam was all that the first Adam was supposed to be—and more.

Yet the new Adam was to experience what the first Adam brought to all his descendants—death. Jesus spoke of himself as "the Son of Man" in texts relating to his impending death (Mark 10:33) and in contexts of human acts of betrayal and perfidy (Luke 22:48). He also spoke of himself as the Son of Man as he explained the central reason for the Incarnation: "For the Son of Man came to seek and to save what was lost" (Luke 19:10).

The Lord spoke of himself as the Son of Man in contexts of Lordship (Matthew 12:8), of final judgment (Matthew 10:23), and of the coming of the glorious kingdom prophesied by the Hebrew prophets (Matthew 16:28). This is a royal designation. The words of the Great Commission began with the gloriously risen One stating that " 'All authority in heaven and on earth has been given to me' " (Matthew 28:18). This is precisely what

Daniel foresaw. It is also akin to the authority given to Adam in the beginning.[12]

So here we have it:

- Christ is the son of Adam (Luke 3:38)
- Christ is the Son of God (Luke 3:22)
- Christ is the last Adam (1 Corinthians 15:45)
- Christ is the Son of Man (Matthew 8:20)

Born to Die

We know that the real issue of the Incarnation is that it was only as Man that God could die. The Christmas cliché—here is One who was born to die—is a vivid reality. While some Christians appear to react too strongly against Christmas in favor of Good Friday and Easter, it is only the cross and the empty tomb that give Christmas its full meaning. May we not see even in the wise men's gifts of frankincense and myrrh (Matthew 2:11) that which portended his death (John 19:39)?

Lower Than the Angels

Now we return to the problem of the quotation of Psalm 8 in Hebrews 2, as promised. The New Testament writer picked the Greek rendering of the central words of the Psalm because they served his purpose. In the context of a growing worship of the angels, the writer of the book wished to elevate the Lord Jesus Christ as the only object of true worship. The world was not going to be ruled by angels in the coming Kingdom but by man, as God promised in Psalm 8:4-6.[13]

Yet it is only as Man that God could die. This seems to be the essential point in the use that Hebrews 2 makes of Psalm 8. In his Incarnation, the Lord Jesus was made lower than the angels, not as a statement of the ignominy of being man, but as a reference to the fact that in becoming man he became subject to death itself:

> But we see Jesus, who was made a little lower than the angels, now crowned with glory and honor

because he suffered death, so that by the grace of
God he might taste death for everyone (Hebrews 2:9).

It is to this end that "heaven came down" in the mystery of
Jesus becoming flesh. Paul has expressed this wonder in words
that may have constituted one of the earliest Christian hymns:

Who, being in very nature God,
    did not consider equality with God something
    to be grasped,
but made himself nothing,
    taking the very nature of a servant,
    being made in human likeness.
And being found in appearance as a man,
    he humbled himself
    and became obedient to death—
    even death on a cross! (Philippians 2:6-8).

There is nothing like the cross of Christ in all the world. It
is the cross of Christ that sets Christianity against all competing
ideologies, religious or secular. "Christian anthropology is an
anthropology of the crucified Lord: it is in relation to this 'Son of
Man' that man recognizes his truth and first becomes true
man."[14]

The Death! of the Savior

In his experience of death, the Man Jesus suffered so intensely that the prophet Isaiah at one point used an intensive
plural (literally "deaths") to describe the horror of that moment
("and with the rich in his death," Isaiah 53:9). Some teachers
have misunderstood this plural and have taught erroneously that
Jesus died in more than one way (body and spirit). The force of
this plural is not numerical, however, but intensive. It is not that
Jesus died twice, but that he DIED.

In the death of the Savior heaven averted its face, darkness
enshrouded the spot—in his death his suffering was such that he
became disfigured and dehumanized:

his appearance was so disfigured
    beyond that of any man
and his form marred
    beyond human likeness (Isaiah 52:14).

The prophet/poet David gave words for the Savior to utter in the excruciation of his pain:

But I am a worm and not a man,
    scorned by men and despised by the people.
                                (Psalm 22:6)

From the Depths

It is in the awfulness of his death that the Lord Jesus was made lower than angels and disfigured in pain below that of humanity itself. But in every text where that horror is described, there are the shouts of victory, the triumph of resurrection, life and exaltation. Psalm 22, which speaks so graphically of the pain of crucifixion (in a day in which crucifixion was not known!), presents as well the promise of his glorious resurrection; the psalmist gives words for the Savior to use as he exults in the name of God among his brethren after God has delivered him from death:

I will declare your name to my brothers;
    in the congregation I will praise you (Psalm 22:22).[15]

Isaiah 53, which portrays the suffering and death of the Savior in unforgettable words, also exudes sheer delight at his victory in life restored:

After the suffering of his soul,
    he will see the light of life and be satisfied.
                                (Isaiah 53:11)[16]

And in Philippians 2 the triumphant sounds of the great hymn of Christian faith animate God's universe:

Therefore God exalted him to the highest place
and gave him the name that is above every name,
that at the name of Jesus every knee should bow,
in heaven and on earth and under the earth,
and every tongue confess that Jesus Christ is Lord,
to the glory of God the Father (Philippians 2:9-
11).

No Limitation

From all these concepts, we may conclude with master
theologian and church historian Geoffrey Bromiley that the true
biblical doctrine of the humanity of the Lord Jesus Christ is not a
limiting factor; it is a new aspect of his great glory.

Finally, the humanity of Christ is not a limiting factor which demands either a restriction or a spasmodic
and paradoxical manifestation of the divine attributes, but a specific form in which the true and living
God can and does bring all His attributes to expression, achieving a unity of person, a communion of
natures, and a communication of attributes, graces,
and operations, without any distortion of humanity
on the one side, or on the other any forfeiture of
deity, whether within the Godhead or in the human
form.[17]

The Savior and Humanism

How can a Christian not be a humanist when the Savior has
become the Son of Man? It is in the Incarnation that God's intention for humanity is realized anew. Psalm 8 points not only back
to the person of first Adam, it points as well to Last Adam, the
Lord Jesus Christ. It is in Jesus that we rediscover what it means
to be human. It is in Jesus that we are drawn near the Father. By
his death on our behalf, we—in him!—come near. Thielicke *is*
correct: Let the adversary rage. When he has declared all that is
awfully true of me and my unworthiness in the presence of God,
Christ interrupts the enemy and addresses the Father:

"What is he then, you ask? He is the one who has accepted me and thus gained the right of sonship that you have promised. Look upon him, then, as you look upon me; he is my brother and your son."[18]

With this view of Christ who is God become Man, we may have an entirely new and enhanced view of our own humanity. As James Hitchcock rightly states, "In the end, Christians are the true humanists."[19]

Chapter 8, Notes

1. Helmut Thielicke, *Being Human . . . Becoming Human* (Garden City, N.Y.: Doubleday, 1984), 76.

2. Hebrew *'adam* (man) is not only etymologically related to Hebrew *'adamah* (earth); Torah makes the connection clear: "for dust you are/ and to dust you will return" (Genesis 3:19).

3. Edmond Jacob, *Theology of the Old Testament*, trans. Arthur W. Heathcote and Philip J. Allcock (New York: Harper & Row, 1958), 152.

4. Ibid.

5. Thielicke, *Being Human*, 85.

6. I have argued that the term translated "unformed body" extends to the embryo from the very moment of conception. This view of God's activity within the womb of the mother should have significant bearing on our thoughts about abortion. See my booklet, *Abortion: When Does Life Begin?* (Portland, Ore.: Multnomah Press, 1984).

7. Harold O. J. Brown, *Heresies: The Image of Christ in the Mirror of Heresy and Orthodoxy from the Apostles to the Present* (Garden City, N.Y.: Doubleday, 1984).

8. Ibid., 7.

9. The Nicene Creed was formulated in 325 by the Council of Nicea, which had been called to deal with the Arian heresy. The Creed serves as a major statement of orthodoxy concerning the Person of Jesus Christ.

10. Brown, *Heresies*, 59.

11. The familiar New Testament expression "only begotten" has been changed in the NIV to "one and only" (as in John 3:16) to emphasize more clearly the basal idea of the Greek term (and the Hebrew concept on which the Greek is derived).

12. An important study of the phrase "the Son of Man" is given by I. Howard Marshall in *The Origins of New Testament Christology* (Leicester: InterVarsity Press, 1976), 63-82. He concludes that the term is "an admirable one for expressing the authority of which Jesus was conscious" (p. 78).

13. These issues are developed well by Donald R. Glenn, "Psalm 8 and Hebrews 2: A Case Study in Biblical Hermeneutics and Biblical Theology," in *Walvoord: A Tribute*, ed. Donald K. Campbell (Chicago: Moody Press, 1982), 43-46.

14. Jürgen Moltmann, *Man: Christian Anthropology in the Conflicts of the Present*, trans. John Sturdy (Philadelphia: Fortress Press, 1974), 20.

15. I find it a matter of beauty that the author of Hebrews quotes Psalm 22:22 in the same context as Psalm 8:4-6 (Hebrews 2:12).

16. In Isaiah 53:11, the NIV follows the reading of I Q Isaiahª, "he will see *the light of life*"; a correct decision in my judgment. The traditional Hebrew text appears to have dropped the object of the verb "to see," leaving an unexpressed object and a considerably weakened testimony of the promise of the resurrection that this verse presents.

17. Geoffrey W. Bromiley, "Christology," in *The International Standard Bible Encyclopedia*, revised ed., ed. G. W. Bromiley, et. al. (Grand Rapids: Wm. B. Eerdmans Publishing Co., 1979), 1:665-66.

18. Thielicke, *Being Human*, 98.

19. James Hitchcock, *What Is Secular Humanism: Why Humanism Became Secular and How It Is Changing Our World* (Ann Arbor, Mich.: Servant Books, 1982), 139.

PART 3

A MANDATE FOR MAN

Gen. 2:24: "and they become one."
We're finally married. It was a long time happening. I
met you such a long time before we got together.
Or so it seemed.
It was love at first sight with me. I remember so
vividly falling into your eyes, tumbling end over end
into their depths. Now my dreams are consummated.
"Be close," says God. "Be closer to one another than
to anyone else in the whole world." I have to practice
this daily, leaving parents, job, children, and
hobbies. To give my mate top priority demands more
than I am by nature willing to give. But the closeness
we feel when I do is worth the effort. I'm glad God
created us to be one flesh.
Closeness means opening up to you, letting you in on
my hidden self, making myself vulnerable to you.
Sometimes I'm afraid you might think me dumb,
foolish, or evil when I reveal myself, but that's the
risk I have to take to insure continuing closeness. I try
to trust you that much.
And it means that I will "pleasure" you. No other
physical delight can touch making love. The touching,
the caressing, the ecstasy all add to the richness of
"cleaving" to each other.
Margaret and Erling Wold
Bible Readings for Couples

Chapter 9

Being Human Together

*I*f learning to state the doctrine of the Person of the Lord Jesus Christ with biblical balance is the principal theological issue that has most troubled the church through time, it may be that the second issue which has most troubled believers is a balanced biblical perspective of male and female. As we saw in the last chapter, the problems concerning the Person of the Savior still confront the church today. As we all know, without reading any chapter, the male and female issue is today more prominent than ever.

The Wrap on Marriage

Contemporary Christian writers on this issue may be found all over the chart (and perhaps a few off the wall?). Think of the contrast, for example, between Marabel Morgan *(The Total Woman)* and Letha Scanzoni *(Sex Is a Parent Affair)*. Is it really possible that women wrapped themselves in the buff in Saran Wrap in order to be the "total woman" for their husbands? And how many were met at the door by other than their husbands? In contrast to Morgan's sensual traditionalism, how will Scanzoni's concept concerning homosexuality as merely a sexual equivalent of lefthandedness (and hence not a moral issue, unless lefthandedness is truly "sinister") affect her thesis that sex is a "parent affair"? That is, what has parenting to do with homosexual marriages?

The Wraps in Print

Consider the range of expression from traditionalist Susan T. Foh *(Women and the Word of God)*, moderate Patricia Gundry *(Woman Be Free, Heirs Together)*, and extremist Virginia Ramey Mollenkott *(The Divine Feminine: The Biblical Imagery of God as Female)*. One thing is for certain: It is hazardous and unfair to generalize on books on feminism by Christian women.

Nor should we restrict our list to women authors. Numerous men have also written in this area, most notably Vernard Eller *(The Language of Canaan and the Grammar of Feminism)*, Donald G. Bloesch *(Is the Bible Sexist?)*, Stephen B. Clark *(Man and Woman in Christ)*, and Paul K. Jewett *(Man as Male and Female)*. Second only to biblical prophecy, the issue of male and female in the Bible and the church has raised considerable ferment in books, lectures, and innumerable discussions. I am fearful that my remarks will be rather modest. Likely the only thing that will please writers I have just mentioned is that I have purchased, read, and cited their books. (May they see at least that one favor deserves another!)

Taking Off the Wraps

For much of its history, the church—like the synagogue—appears to have been uncomfortable with the issue of human sexuality. Because of the ever present abuse of sexuality in many cultures of the world, the church has at times seemed to keep the issue under wraps. This is not to say that the church has ignored sexuality. Christians have participated in God's gifts; Christians too have babies. But Christians have not always felt comfortable in talking about the matter. Not until recently. Now it seems this is all some ever talk about! One of the most uproarious "Phil Donahue" programs I remember seeing was one that featured several leading representatives of the evangelical sexual renaissance. I'm not sure if even Donahue, himself no stranger to talk show themes relating to sexuality, was prepared for the ribald likes of the Reverend Doctor Charles Shedd!

Forbidden Song

I recall two experiences as a young theologue, both related to the biblical book on human sexuality, the Song of Solomon. When I was a high school student I heard a series of radio messages on this Old Testament book by an exceptionally able and well-known Bible scholar, a man for whom I have abiding respect. I recently had the occasion to listen to a tape of one of those messages from years ago. I listened this time with my Bible open and discovered something that I somehow had missed back then. In his messages from chapter 8, he read the chapter but omitted verses 1, 3, 8, and 10, verses that speak of breasts and lovemaking in explicit terms. His message of Christ's love for the church was not hindered by the omission of these verses.

The other experience occurred nearly twenty years ago—that long?—when I was preparing to go to seminary. My pastor may have run a considerable risk by asking me to prepare and preach a sermon as a part of my going-away festivities. I remember selecting Song of Solomon chapter 1 for my text and working very hard on my message. I suspect that the ratio of hours of study to minutes of presentation was higher for that one message than for any I have preached since. Unencumbered by hermeneutics (the task of proper interpretation), unentangled by sense of literary genre, I blithely presented a message of salvation and redemption from that wonderful chapter of Scripture. The words "dark am I, yet lovely" (1:5) were to me a strong statement of a forgiven sinner loved by the Savior despite his past. I took as a compliment the words of an elder in the church, "You really did a marvelous job in getting that message from that passage! How did you do it?" As I think of that message twenty years later—well, I have heard worse.

Learning to Sing

But a change has come in evangelical circles in the last two decades, a change that has much that is good in it. The reticence of the beloved radio scholar and the ignorance of my own youth need not be maintained by Bible teachers or lay students in our day. Evangelicals have discovered biblical sexuality and have found that it is good.

> Sensuous love with erotic overtones is God's intent
> for the marriage relationship. The distortion of that
> relationship has no doubt abased this dimension of
> life, but that does not justify placing such expe-
> rience—or Scripture's Song about it—into the inac-
> tive file of living.[1]

Joseph Dillow's book, *Solomon on Sex,* combines a literal presentation of the message of the Song with a brief marriage manual for the Christian couple. The fact that an entire book of the Bible, the Song of Solomon, is devoted to the beauty of erotic love as God's gift to a man and a woman is still to be realized by many Christians in our day.

An author friend of mine tells me of a rejection notice he received from a fine Christian publishing house. The stated reason for the rejection was a chapter in his manuscript that presents the Song of Solomon as a tract for loving couples. In the judgment of that house, their public was not ready for such a view. The mystical and allegorical interpretations of the Song have a long history in the synagogue and in the church and were culturally conditioned. But this tradition is, in my judgment, a rebuke against sound scholarship and a retreat from truly biblical thinking—which will be maintained in our own day only at our peril. Biblically oriented Christians should no more leave the discussion of human sexuality to the Hefners and Friedans of our age than we should leave the study of science to Carl Sagan.

Showman of Science

We should not leave the discussion of sexuality to Carl Sagan either. Sagan, famed Cornell University astronomer and the host of the public television series *Cosmos,* is a gifted communicator and an enthusiast for science with such a flair that *Time* magazine featured him in a cover story (20 October 1980), under the title "The Cosmic Explainer." In that article Sagan rhapsodized, "Science is a joy. It is not just something for an isolated, remote elite. It is our birthright."[2] With this ebullient statement we should be in profound agreement, as we shall see in a later chapter.

But there is more to Carl Sagan than just an infectious love for science. There is as well a determined nontheistic religiosity to his work. As Christ has his apostles, Sagan is something of an apostle for nontheistic evolution. The opening words of his beautifully produced volume, *Cosmos,* serve as parody to Scripture: "The Cosmos is all that is or ever was or ever will be."[3] His use of the capital in the word "Cosmos" betrays his new deity.[4] Here is Sagan's deliberate denial of Genesis 1:1 and John 1:1 and his studied contempt for the words of the angelic beings in the heavenly court who say of God, the Creator of the universe, that it is he "who was, and is, and is to come" (Revelation 4:8).

The Great Discovery

Nowhere is Sagan's audacity more apparent than in his assumption concerning the origin of sexuality in living forms. He describes the earth of four billion years ago as "a molecular Garden of Eden," and that by three billion years ago the first multicellular organisms had evolved. Then comes the sorcerer's magic: "Sex seems to have been invented around two billion years ago."[5]

That Sagan's blasé statement is merely magic is shown in an article in the popular magazine of science, *Discovery.* In an essay on the origin of sex in evolutionary theory, the authors state that many biologists are really quite puzzled as to why nature would choose sexual reproduction. Sex is viewed as an inefficient and risky way for organisms to reproduce themselves. Asexual reproduction (parthenogenesis) is considered a more likely choice for nature to make: "It is faster and more efficient, and it allows a creature both to replicate itself without the bother of mating, and to produce offspring that carry all of its genes."[6] Among evolutionary authorities quoted by the authors, George Williams, population biologist of the State University of New York at Stony Brook, says, "At first glance, and second, and third, it appears that sex shouldn't have evolved."[7]

Something Missing

But why then is there sex?

In the end, the offhand answer to the question, "Why sex?—Why not?"—seems not quite so flip. Are biologists any closer to an answer than they were fifty years ago? Perhaps not. Says John Maynard Smith of the University of Sussex, in England, one of the leading students of the mystery, "One is left with the feeling that some essential feature of the situation is being overlooked."[8]

Indeed! Whether it is Carl Sagan or John Maynard Smith, some essential feature of the situation is being overlooked—Yahweh himself! When it comes to the human species, we may declare, not with magic but with revelation from the Creator, that sexuality in the human species was designed by God to allow man as male and female to be truly human. In fact, the mystery and companionship of genuine human sexuality may become a significant element in the argument from design (teleology) for the existence of God. The now well-known factor of incongruent curves of sexual response for the man and the woman, the absence of a rutting season as in many of the animals, the discovery that the woman's clitoris is a specific organ for sexual pleasure—these data all lead to a view of transcendence in human sexuality.

The impulse that looks only for its own satisfaction, as a kind of end in itself, fails to achieve it. This special element in human sexuality sets us the task of transcending nature. Creatureliness means that we are constantly summoned to move toward a goal, the specifically human element, that goes beyond natural factors. This applies even to the corporeal side. The body with its libido represents us. Being human, we are made for communication. We live for and by others. We are meant to serve and be served. This is true even in the sphere in which the body represents us.[9]

A Moment before Eve

Think again of the simple but profound story in Genesis 2. In this account of the formation of man, the greatest of the creatures made by Yahweh God, the male was formed first without a suitable partner to aid and share with him life and service to God. The parading of all the other creatures before the male demonstrated several features of his creation:

- The man was magnificently gifted with intelligence, speech, scientific inquiry, insight, and wonder.
- The man was not unaware of the coupling patterns of the creatures he investigated.
- The man found himself to be alone even while he was surrounded by God's rich and varied creation.
- His discovery of the unhappiness of loneliness was a confirmation of the word of the Creator that such a condition was "not good" (Genesis 2:18).
- When God formed of the man's own substance that feminine partner truly corresponding to him and altogether fitting for him, the man's response was one of exquisite joy (Genesis 2:23).
- The plain meaning of the text of the creation story is that the celebration of the joy of togetherness was in the wonderful discovery of the sexual embrace. This is the certain testimony of the editorial remarks of Genesis 2:24,

> For this reason a man will leave his father and
> mother and be united to his wife, and they will
> become one flesh.

It is also the demand of the narrative conclusion
of Genesis 2:25,

> The man and his wife were both naked, and
> they felt no shame.

Not a "No-No"

There are still many well-meaning people who have the
mistaken notion that the forbidden fruit of the Fall was the discovery of sex—the necessary "no-no" of our existence. Yet the
fall of man was not in our first parents' "playing doctor," any
more than it was merely a dietary infringement. The summary
words of Genesis 2:24 are inserted by the narrator to answer the
major question concerning the origin of our powerful sexual
drive. Where does the potent force of our human sexuality come
from, this force which is "strong as death" (Song 8:6)?

> It comes from the fact that God took woman from
> man, that they actually were originally one flesh.
> Therefore they must come together again and thus by
> destiny they belong to each other.[10]

For these reasons the writers of the Hebrew Scriptures
never reacted against human sexuality as did some later purist
sects in Greece, and some misdirected Jewish and Christian
groups through time. "In Israel there is a certain balance between the natural and the spiritual element in sexual life; this is
only possible owing to the fact that in Yahweh power over nature and moral being were completely fused."[11]

Together as Male and Female

A basic biblical teaching, then, on the meaning of man is
the meaning of man as male and female together. "True human
life is life together, and a life of isolation is a perversion of
human nature as divinely created."[12]

This is the way the Song of Songs should be read. The title of that book is not a Hebrew pleonasm (the use of more words than necessary); it is a superlative. One might speak of this book as "The Most Beautiful Song." It is true! The most beautiful song in the Bible is a song about human love.

Recently I spoke at a Valentine's banquet for couples in my church. I am sure that I surprised them, because I broke from the expected liturgy of such services. You know how those things go. Couples come to a nice restaurant to enjoy a splendid dinner with dear friends. They sing sentimental songs of love, with the lights down low in the room. There are some funny skits that point out the human foibles in love. Then there is special music, moving from romantic songs to spiritual hymns, leading to the message—which is supposed to be on the love of God. I broke the pattern, for while I did not ignore the love of God, I spoke particularly on the love of man and woman as described in the Bible. (See what can happen in twenty years?)

More Than Eagles

The biblical view of human sexuality, God's great gift to man in majesty, is that it is too amazing for any of us to comprehend but it ought to result in great praise to God. The learned sage Agur used numerical parallelism to describe his own sense of wonder at natural phenomena, where the last numbered is the supernal surprise:

> There are three things that are too amazing for me,
>   four that I do not understand:
> the way of an eagle in the sky,
>   the way of a snake on a rock,
> the way of a ship on the high seas,
>   and the way of a man with a maiden.
>   (Proverbs 30:18-19)

The concept of the loving caresses of a man and a woman transcends the wonder of the flight of eagles, movement of snakes, and the sailing of ships. It is, as Paul confesses, the ultimate mystery (Ephesians 5:32; note the quotation he makes of

Genesis 2:24 in that context). If you, the reader of these words, are married and struggling with your own concept of your physical relationship to your mate, may I encourage the both of you to read together the words of the Most Beautiful Song. Read them in the New International Version or in the New King James Version, where the characters are specified. Discover that the phrase "the rose of Sharon" (Song 2:1) is not a name of Jesus, but a description of the beloved woman. As you read the words, read them all. Do not omit verses as my radio preacher did so long ago! Recapture for yourselves the biblical joy of human sex, accepted by loving couples in praise of God.

Madam Folly Destroys the Fun

The world is so confused about these issues. In a vacuum of positive teaching concerning biblical sexuality, the culture of our day has become obsessed with sex. But the sexuality of the world is not enjoyed in the praise of God. Sexuality in the world is that of Madam Folly whose slatternly call to passersby is a parody of Lady Wisdom. Whereas Wisdom presents a luxurious banquet (Proverbs 9:1-6) which is the food of life, that old slut Folly says:

"Stolen water is sweet;
 food eaten in secret is delicious!" (Proverbs 9:17).

Any fool knows that these words are a call for illicit sexual relationships.[13] These are the things that animate the fantasies of soap operas and paperback romances. Once our appetites are stimulated for "stolen waters," our desires become more insatiable and more bizarre, leading to the depraved societal ills of which we are all too familiar (and which are as old as Leviticus 18 and Romans 1). Why should the *Playboy* philosophy destroy fun, dehumanize women, and cheapen God's gift?

What Happened?

Where then did things go wrong? How did human sexuality become the source of so much of our evil, so much of our pain, so much of our discontent? What happened to our parents when they went east of Eden?

Genesis 3:15 has long been given great attention by learned scholars and simple Bible readers alike. These words are sometimes called *protoeuangelion,* the "first gospel," but they are words of judgment on the serpent, the provocateur of rebellion:

> "And I will put enmity
> > between you and the woman,
> > and between your offspring and hers;
> he will crush your head,
> > and you will strike his heel."

Words to Our Mother Eve

In our enthusiasm over these words of Genesis 3:15, which Eve anticipated might be fulfilled even in the birth of her first son Cain,[14] we may not have given sufficient attention to the next verse and its implications for trouble ahead:

> To the woman he said,
> > "I will greatly increase your pains in childbearing;
> > > with pain you will give birth to children.
> > Your desire will be for your husband,
> > > and he will rule over you" (Genesis 3:16).

Two interpretational errors have been made on the basis of this verse. One error is to state that the woman's sexual desire is a part of her curse; the other is to suggest that the man's rule over the woman is a result of sin. John Davis, for example, in a popular exposition of the Book of Genesis seems to perpetuate both errors. He speaks of three effects of the Fall on the woman: (1) her sorrow of conception, (2) her deep natural attraction for her husband, and (3) her rule by the man.[15] Davis is not alone in this analysis of Genesis 3:16. Even the sophisticated commentary by Gerhard von Rad speaks of three facts grinding down the woman's life.[16]

Time for a Closer Look

We may avoid these errors by judging rightly the nature of the parallelism of this verse. A poetic analysis of the verse suggests the following arrangement (in personal translation):

(1) An introductory monocolon:
"To the woman he said."

(2) One synonymous bicolon:
"I will most certainly multiply (!)
your pain in childbirth;
In pain you shall bring forth children."

(3) One antithetical bicolon:
"And to your husband shall your desire be,
But he shall rule over you."

Labor Pains

It is clear from the structure of the verse itself that there are two results of the Fall on woman, not three. The first result is pain in childbirth.[17] We may presume on the basis of this verse that had the Fall not occurred, the bearing of children would have been without the pain so many women experience. A word of caution is in order here. I have heard some men say that any attempt to reduce the pain in childbearing (by anesthesia or by muscle and breathing preparation) is an affront to the curse. Somehow these same men find no affront to the curse on the man respecting sweat on the brow (Genesis 3:19) in their use of labor-saving equipment, not to mention gloves and potions to handle the thorns (3:18).

Compensating Desire?

The second result of the Fall affecting the woman is given in the antithetical bicolon at the end of the verse:
"Your desire will be for your husband,
and he will rule over you."

The interpretation of this passage poses some difficulties, as we will discover. But the interpretation that Davis (and others) suggests, that a woman's sexual desire for her husband is a result of the Fall,[18] is offensive to women and is an affront to biblical sexuality and the Creator's design. (Here is good reason indeed for the training of more women exegetes and theologians.)

Are we to understand that before the Fall the woman was so designed by God that she would have no sexual desire for her husband? If her sexual desire is a part of her curse, does this not suggest the physical embrace is a compensation for the pain of childbearing? Is this text to be taken as a "bad news good news" burlesque—that God was giving her pain, but compensatory pleasure? Are we to understand that sexual desire was pronounced "good" only when exercised by the man, but a "compensation" when experienced by the woman? These questions suggest that the viewpoint prompting them is alien to the concept of sexuality presented in the Bible. It is an exegetical error to term the sexual desire of the woman a result of the Fall.

A second interpretational error made by some otherwise fine commentators on this passage is the assertion that the rule of the man over the woman is likewise a result of the Fall. Even Luther suggested this point of view when he said, "Had Eve not sinned she would [not] . . . have been subject to her husband."[19]

Yet we saw earlier in this book (chapter 6) that there is a principle of leadership for the man over the woman that results from his priority in creation and his role in naming the woman. If these writers intend that the concept of the subjection of the woman to the man (as in Ephesians 5:22) is the result of the Fall, then this earlier observation must be discounted. On the other hand, perhaps more is intended in the words "he will rule over you" than we first might think. The Jerusalem Bible may point the way in its stronger translation, "he will lord it over you."

Let's Look Again

We have already suggested that the words of this bicolon should be read antithetically:

> And to your husband shall your desire be,
> *But* he shall rule over you.

Yet how shall we understand this couplet? Several years ago I came across an article in the *Westminster Theological Journal* by Susan T. Foh that points in a new and satisfying direction. The key term in our passage is the Hebrew word *t ᵉšûqâ*, "desire, longing." This is a rare word, found only three times in the Old Testament. Moreover, the etymology of this term is uncertain. Its root generally has been believed to be related to the Arabic word *šawq*, "desire," and the directionality would be in *sexual* desire. However, because of noncorresponding sibilants, Foh suggests that the preferable Arabic cognate is *sāqa*, "to urge, drive on, impel." This suggestion removes sexual connotations from the curse altogether.[20]

A Word to Cain

A second passage in which this debated word *t ᵉšûqâ* is found is Genesis 4:7, in God's words of warning to Cain:

"If you do what is right, will you not be accepted?
But if you do not do what is right, sin is crouching
at your door;
    it [sin] desires to have you,
    but you [Cain] must master it."

While not evident perhaps in translation, the Hebrew text of Genesis 4:7b is precisely the same as that in Genesis 3:16b, with appropriate changes for person and gender. Foh observes that God speaks in Genesis 4:7 of the desire of sin to enslave Cain, but that if he were actively and decisively to struggle against it, he would be able to master sin in his life. She then argues that Genesis 3:16 may be informed from this more obvious struggle in the case of Cain. In the relationship between the woman and the man in the days following the Fall, there is an ongoing struggle for leadership. "These words," Foh says, "mark the beginning of the battle of the sexes."[21] I do not follow Foh, however, when she suggests that God commands the man to dominate his mate: "he must fight for his headship."[22] Rather, the implication of Genesis 3:16 is that the man will tend to be as loveless as the woman is nonsubmissive.

A Paraphrase

An expanded paraphrase of Genesis 3:16 would read something like the following:

God then spoke to the woman as a consequence of her rebellion against the beneficent rule of Yahweh, the following new realities that shall mark her life:
> I will bring something new into the wonder of the bringing of children into the world.
>> I will greatly magnify your pain in giving birth.
>> When you give birth to your children it will be in physical pain.
> I will also allow pain to come into your marriage relationship with your husband.
>> You will tend to desire to usurp the role I have given to him as the compassionate leader in your home, rejecting his role and belittling his manhood.
>> And the man on his part will tend to relate to you in loveless tyranny, dominating and stifling your integrity as an equal partner to himself.

No Wonder

If this is an accurate reflection of the intention of this curse on the woman, it is a curse indeed that has lasted through time. No wonder there is such discord among married couples. No wonder there is such ferment among women—and men! No wonder we all question the very meaning of being male and female. No wonder some people attempt today to deny even the most obvious differences between the sexes and slip more and more into homosexual and bisexual behavior. Think of the trends toward unisexual clothing in some subcultures. Observe particularly some rock music stars with their calculated transvestism.

New Hope in Christ

If the interpretation I have suggested is correct, it also points to great hope for the believing couple. The man and the woman who know the power of Christ—the New Adam—can call upon his power to reverse the effects of the Fall as they relate to each other. This, I believe, is the force of the text in Ephesians that is used mistakenly so many times by men to put down women. Instead of being a general statement on proper sexual roles, Ephesians 5 is a specific answer to the problems of couples living east of Eden.

Reversing the Roles

When Paul says to the woman that she is to submit to her husband (Ephesians 5:22), he is reversing the new inclination that came with the Fall; the woman does not wish to submit to him at all, but to struggle against his leadership and to usurp his role in their home. The apostle, who is accused too often (and unfairly) of hating women, shows here his true concern for the woman. When he says that she must submit to her husband, it is not with a grin-and-bear-it attitude, receiving each stroke from her sadistic mate as a love caress from God. Further, it is most certainly not because her husband is a hammer of the Lord beating on her, the chisel, so that she in turn may chip away on their children. Such an image, which has been made repeatedly by the enormously popular teaching of a major seminar leader in America, must be challenged by believing men and women as unfitting of the teaching of the Word of God.

No! The woman is directed by the apostle Paul to submit to her husband not as a chisel to a hammer, but as the church to the Savior. The woman may learn to submit to the leadership of her husband because she may see in him (by her great faith!) one who reflects the Person of the Lord Jesus Christ himself. Only a very high view of women on the part of the apostle, and the Lord who gave this word through him, would make such a suggestion possible. Moreover, the woman's submission to the man is in the context of mutual submission (5:21), ruling out the east-of-Eden domination that many people envision.

Not as Tarzan, but as Christ

And the husband, whose natural bent since the Fall has been to behave as a brute toward his wife, is told by Paul that he is to be for her as Christ! The man is not to dominate and subjugate and stifle his wife. He is to love her. Love her as Christ loved her. Sacrifice for her. Give his all for her. Die for her!

Where in this image is the hammer pounding on the chisel, which in turn is chipping on the children? Away with that idea, along with all views of mistreatment of women by abusing husbands—no matter who the teacher is.

Ephesians 5:21-33 is a bouleversement, a full reversal of the conditions in the home brought about by the Fall of man as male and female. It is possible for the Christian home to recapture a bit of Eden. When the man loves his wife as Christ loves the church, and she sees that quality in him, she will be able to resist the east-of-Eden urge to put him in his place. And when the man senses her shared life with him as the royal prerogative of man in majesty, his love for her will abound, and he will be able to resist his own east-of-Eden urge to grab the club, swell the chest, and say "Me Tarzan; you Jane."

There will still be thorns on the roses and pain with birthing—but man as male and female may by Christ's power live their lives in true majesty on this side of glory. May this be true, dear reader, for you and for me.

In our marriages, let us exalt the last Adam, the Lord Jesus Christ. Let us be truly human together!

Chapter 9, Notes

1. Howard G. Hendricks, Foreword to *A Song for Lovers* by S. Craig Glickman (Downers Grove, Ill.: InterVarsity Press, 1976), 9.

2. Frederic Golden, "The Cosmic Explainer," *Time*, 20 October 1980, 69.

3. Carl Sagan, *Cosmos* (New York: Random House, 1980), 4.

4. Richard A. Baer, Jr., another Cornell University scientist, comes to the same conclusion in "They *Are* Teaching Religion in the Public Schools," *Christianity Today*, 17 February 1984, 12-15. Baer states: "In fact, Sagan's stance in 'Cosmos' is thoroughly religious. It is simply that it is a *different* religion from that of Christianity or Judaism" (p. 13).

5. Sagan, *Cosmos*, 31.

6. Gina Maranto and Shannon Brownlee, "Why Sex?" *Discovery*, February 1984, 24.

7. Ibid.

8. Ibid., 28.

9. Helmut Thielicke, *Being Human . . . Becoming Human* (Garden City, N.Y.: Doubleday, 1984), 195.

10. Gerhard von Rad, *Genesis: A Commentary*, trans. John H. Marks (Philadelphia: The Westminster Press, 1961), 82-83.

11. Th. C. Vriezen, *An Outline of Old Testament Theology*, 2d. ed. (Newton, Mass.: Charles T. Branford Co., 1970), 341.

12. William Sanford La Sor, David Allen Hubbard and Frederic William Bush, *Old Testament Survey: The Message, Form, and Background of the Old Testament* (Grand Rapids: Wm. B. Eerdmans Publishing Co., 1982), 79.

13. Cf. James L. Crenshaw, *Old Testament Wisdom: An Introduction* (Atlanta: John Knox Press, 1981), 98.

14. Eve's words in Genesis 4:1 may be translated, "I have brought forth a man—Yahweh"; her (mistaken) belief that the words of promise of Genesis 3:15 were about to be realized in her son Cain. This view of Luther is supported by Walter C. Kaiser, Jr., *Toward an Old Testament Theology* (Grand Rapids: Zondervan Publishing House, 1978), 37.

15. John J. Davis, *Paradise to Prison: Studies in Genesis* (Grand Rapids: Baker Book House, 1975), 93-94. No particular acrimony toward the distinguished professor of Old Testament at Grace Theological Seminary is intended by these observations. Any number of commentaries might reveal much the same approach.

16. Von Rad, *Genesis*, 90.

17. The KJV rendering, "thy sorrow and thy conception" is possible, and is defended by Cassuto (see U. Cassuto, *A Commentary on the Book of Genesis, Part I: From Adam to Noah*, trans. Israel Abrahams [Jerusalem: The Magnes Press, The Hebrew University, 1961], 165). This suggests that a woman is to have constant sorrow in general, but particularly difficult pain in the bearing of children. This seems, however, an especially dour view of woman (although some might feel that it has been their experience!). It seems preferable for us to regard the words "pain and childbearing" as an example of hendiadys (one concept expressed through two terms): "your pains in childbearing" (NIV); or "your pain in childbirth" (NASB).

18. This point of view is found often, and sometimes in misogynic degrees. These are the words of Harold Stigers: "Now, she herself finds the psychological balance overturned against her; she will find within herself a yearning for man which on occasion amounts to nymphomania" (Harold G. Stigers, *A Commentary on Genesis* [Grand Rapids: Zondervan Publishing House, 1976], 80). Gasp! A similar strident statement is given by H. C. Leupold. He describes the yearning of the woman for the man as "morbid" and states, "It may be normal. It often is not but takes a perverted form, even to the point of nymphomania. It is a just penalty" (H. C. Leupold, *Exposition of Genesis*, 2 vols. [Grand Rapids: Baker Book House, 1942], 1:172). This may be an unkind remark, but did these writers have their wives proofread for them?

Davis's wording of the nature of the curse on the woman seems to mitigate against this point of view. He says, "The wife would have a deep natural attraction for her husband" (Davis, *Genesis*, 94). The word "natural" is consequent neither with Stigers's suggestion of "nymphomania" nor the context of malediction in which this text must be explained, even though von Rad feels both "curse" and "malediction" are terms too strong for the "severe afflictions and terrible contradiction that now break upon the woman's life" (von Rad, *Genesis*, 91).

19. Martin Luther, *Commentary on Genesis,* 2 vols. trans. J. Theodore Mueller (Grand Rapids: Zondervan Publishing House, 1958), 1:82.

20. Susan T. Foh, "What Is the Woman's Desire?" *Westminster Theological Journal* 37 (Spring 1975): 380-81. She has summarized this article in her book, *Woman and the Word of God* (Grand Rapids: Baker Book House, 1979), 67-69. The third use of this noun is in Song 7:10 where the woman says of her beloved, "I am my beloved's and his *desire* is for me." In this context, the word is surely sexual in direction.

21. Foh, "Woman's Desire," 381-82.

22. Ibid., 382.

All wisdom comes from the Lord
and is with him forever.
The sand of the sea and the drops of rain
and the days of old—who can count them?
The height of heaven and the breadth of the earth,
the underworld and wisdom—who can penetrate them?
Wisdom was created before all things,
and clever insight is from the beginning of time.
The root of wisdom—to whom has it been revealed?
Her cleverness—who knows it?
There is one who is wise, greatly to be feared,
sitting upon his throne, the Lord.
He created her, saw her and numbered her,
and poured her out upon all his works.
She dwells with all flesh according to his gift,
and he gives her to those who fear him.
Sirach
Ecclesiasticus

. . . the mystery of God, namely, Christ,
in whom are hidden all the treasures
of wisdom and knowledge.
The Apostle Paul

Chapter 10

Being Human in Wisdom

*I*n October 1512, five years before Martin Luther was to begin to shake the very foundations of the Roman Catholic Church, the great Renaissance painter and humanist Michelangelo had just finished decorating one of its ceilings.

And what a ceiling it was! The Sistine Chapel in Rome, named for Pope Sixtus IV who had begun its construction in 1473, has a ceiling that measures approximately 133 feet by 43 feet, with the crown of the vault some 70 feet above the pavement. In conditions of terrible discomfort, the great artist Michelangelo spent nearly four years painting in the fresh plaster on the ceiling. He lay on hard scaffolding boards, breathing intolerable air and having eyes and skin constantly inflamed with plaster dust. All the while, the impatient Pope Julius II would periodically climb the scaffolding and threaten to toss the master to the ground if he did not finish his work more quickly.

Holding Hands with Humanism

The formal unveiling took place on 31 October 1512. What an event in the history of man this unveiling was—one of the finest artistic achievements of the Renaissance. Here Christian theology and humanism learned to hold hands. In his recital of the significance of this event, Charles H. Morgan says that Michelangelo "had joined two powerful philosophies, the Christian ethic and the perfect human, at the moment of their most sympathetic coexistence."[1]

This blending of the Christian and the human strains was perhaps nowhere more evident than in Michelangelo's portrayal of the Creation of Man. One of the most famous panels of the masterpiece is the scene of Adam reclining inertly on a brown field, his left arm stretched out languidly over his upraised left knee. Rushing toward him is God, surrounded by storm and cloud, attended by cherubim, and stretching out his hand in a dynamic gesture to the extended finger of Adam. Our attention is drawn to the rushing power of the finger of God and the small space left between God's finger and that of man. In this painting, we are there a microsecond before the giving of life!

What are we to make of this imagery? Morgan sees in it the notion that the church had given nourishment to humanism and that in this painting they both meet on an equal scale. Despite the tranquility of the scene, Morgan senses the irony in the painting, for a struggle was about to burst out between the church and humanism in which the power of God would be challenged by man whom heaven had empowered.[2]

The Woman at God's Side

Another view of the significance of the Creation of Man fresco is presented by the renowned American biblical theologian Samuel Terrien of Union Seminary, New York. Dr. Terrien, in a meeting of the Society of Biblical Literature in San Francisco several years ago, observed that there is another figure in the painting in addition to God, Adam, and the cherubim. This other figure is a beautiful woman whose head is nestled in the left arm of God, and who looks with anxious interest on man whom God was enlivening.

We almost miss this woman because of our interest in the latent energy in the space between the finger of Adam and the finger of God. But there she is! And her presence causes us to ask, Who is she? Is she the as yet unformed Eve, awaiting the awakening of need for her in her mate? Is she, as some Catholics have imagined, the Blessed Virgin Mary, anticipating a significant day long in the future when God would have a ministry of mystery for her? Terrien brushes away these and other conceptions with his great discovery: This woman is wisdom. It was with his arm around wisdom that God created man, his finest creature.[3]

I suspect that Morgan's point of view more accurately represents art history. But I am convinced that the viewpoint of Terrien is the one we need in order to understand theology rightly. For this painting points us to one of the most significant elements in our understanding of what it means to be truly human: *We were created by God to be wise.*

In this chapter we shall follow the great insight of Michelangelo as interpreted by Terrien. We will learn something of the nature of the wisdom literature in the Hebrew Bible, and something of Lady Wisdom who was at God's side when he created our father Adam.

Biblical Wisdom—the Land to the West

We have come a long way in our study of Psalm 8 and its implications. Our study of this poem has led us first back to the story in Genesis 1 and 2 of the original creation of man as male and female. There we learned anew that man as male and female was made in the image of God in order to reflect his majesty upon the earth he had made. But man rebelled against his God. We cannot consider our own creation apart from our Fall, for man as male and female is profoundly fallen, even though he still bears the image of God as his birthmark. Our study has taken us into the future to consider the nature of the Lord Jesus Christ, the last Adam who reclaims for us what it means to be truly human. We have had to deal as well with the issues of the male and female relationship, one of the most controversial concepts of our day. In that study we learned that it is in Christ that we learn to relate to each other as male and female.

Now we are driven by Psalm 8 to explore biblical wisdom, for it is in the wisdom literature of the Bible that we learn of the role God desires wisdom to have in our lives. Psalm 8 is a wisdom psalm, and as such is a part of the wisdom literature of the Old Testament. But to mention wisdom literature may be to make some people a bit edgy. For some, the biblical wisdom literature is sort of the Wild West of the Hebrew Scriptures. It is largely uncharted, is rumored to be filled with savages, and is (or so we suspect) inhospitable to readers more used to Torah and Gospel. But this is a land to be explored not only because it is there, but because it has treasures of great value. Moreover, it has an organic relationship to the more familiar territory. It may be that our very survival will depend on how well we grasp wisdom literature. For our model in wisdom is the Lord Jesus himself.

Behold the Maxim

Let's take a moment or two to give a rough chart to the wildlands of the Book of Proverbs, the centerpiece of biblical wisdom literature. When we turn to the Book of Proverbs, we find that it contains two basic types of literature. One type is the short maxim. This is what we would expect from the very title of the book. Most of us have a concept of the proverb learned as a part of growing up. In fact, a help to growing up is one of the principal functions of proverbs in many cultures of the world. These are pegs for living that help us arrange our lives in an orderly manner.

Proverbs are likely to be found in nearly every culture of the world. Though some peoples use proverbs more than others, the making of proverbs is a common human activity. Our own English language has a rich heritage of proverbs, such as the familiar words, "A stitch in time saves nine." The idea of this humble proverb is readily apparent and it is transferable to many human tasks.

African tribal heritages are luxuriant with proverbs.[4] Here is one from the Bakongo people of Zaire: "No lion chasing after a wild deer would abandon the hunt to track down a caterpillar." One does not have to live in the bush to see the appropriateness and the transferable truth of this proverb. The most sophisticated nuclear physicist in Moscow would understand this, as would his or her counterpart in North Carolina.

Folk Wisdom and God's Breath

Here is an example of the typical proverb within the ancient Hebrew collection:

> An anxious heart weighs a man down,
>   but a kind word cheers him up (Proverbs 12:25).

This type of proverb is a part of world folk literature. These proverbs are based on experience and reflection and are stated briefly and memorably. In this brief maxim is a description of attitudes that has many applications. The poetic form allows for crafting and memorization; the contrasting parallelism develops the thoughts more forcefully than either element given alone. The basic idea of this proverb is clear: anxiety can bring a man down, a friendly word may lift him up. However, there are people who make more of the proverbs than they should. To make them say more than they really do say is to make them less by despising what they are.

We need to learn how to interpret these proverbs rightly. Some tend to read all parts of the Bible in the same way; they read Isaiah in the same way as they read Ephesians. We simply cannot expect to read the Book of Proverbs with the same expectations as we might read a New Testament epistle or an Old Testament prophet. The proverbs of the Old Testament are not doctrinal formulations, but practical applications. These are not prophecies, but proverbs; they are not categorical, but general. Nevertheless, the proverbs are true and they are a part of the Scriptures that have been breathed-out by God (2 Timothy 3:16-17). The proverbs in the Bible are of great importance for all who desire to live well the life of faith, for they tell us how countless numbers of God's people in the past have learned how God's world works. They help us learn to live our lives in this world with a measure of harmony.

The Center: The Fear of Yahweh

The distinctive character of the proverbs in the Bible is that they all relate to the basic concept in biblical wisdom literature—*the fear of Yahweh*. Proverbs 1:7 is more than a motto of the book:

> The fear of the LORD is the beginning of knowledge,
> but fools despise wisdom and discipline.

These words speak of the basic foundation for true wisdom and of its ongoing structure. Proverbial statements in other cultures are likely to be true, for they have presumably stood the test of time and experience within the culture of that people. But what if a given culture has values that are not really good, that are not truly in accord with biblical revelation? What if a culture values treachery as Don Richardson found in his early experiences in Irian Jaya? Proverbs that might speak of the good of treachery would be true to that culture, but false to God and Gospel. Judas becomes a hero and Jesus a wimp.

The proverbs in the Bible are certainly true and utterly trustworthy because they are based in and structured by the fear of Yahweh. This concept is the heart of wisdom in the Bible. The fear of Yahweh is not a terror before him, but a positive response to his majesty and glory, a readiness to worship and serve him, a recognition of who he is and who man is before him. When the writer of Psalm 8 speaks of the majesty of man, it is in the context of the fear of Yahweh and with due regard to his great glory. This is the reason for the frame of praise to God in verses 1 and 9; only in that frame does the central picture of the praise of man make sense.

The Other Face of Wisdom

A very different type of literature is also found in the Book of Proverbs. In addition to the maxim, there is extended instruction literature, such as the section we find in Proverbs 1-9. These first nine chapters of the book are a connected whole; we need to read them as a continuing poetic discourse. Here the context for the instructional section is as in other books of the Bible, in the flow of the text and its setting. In contrast, the one-verse maxims seem to have little organization to them. The context for the one or two verse maxim is not to be found in the expected surrounding verses but in the verses that deal with the same topic, no matter where in the book they may be found.

The writing of a proverb was a craft of the folk; the writing of the wisdom instruction of Proverbs 1-9 was truly art. It was also great theology.

Lady Wisdom and Madam Folly

It is in Proverbs 1-9 that the wisdom writer presents the stunning personification of wisdom as a woman. It is also here that folly is personified as a woman, but a woman of a different sort! Wisdom is a Lady—as beautiful and desirable as she is chaste. Lady Wisdom offers herself to passersby as a gift of life. Madam Folly is a slatternly harlot whose gifts are guilt, disease, and death itself. This pitiable creature is a ghastly parody of wisdom. But while she is a hag, she is not to be trifled with: Her teeth may be false but her venomous bite is deadly. (We saw something of the contrast between these two women in our last chapter, as we contrasted the banquets of Lady Wisdom and Madam Folly in Proverbs 9.)

Lady Wisdom at Her Finest

The high point of the theology of the Book of Proverbs is in chapter 8. It is in this chapter that the poet reaches his greatest artistic height, and it is here that the meaning is most significant for our understanding of ourselves as the men and women of God's creation.

This is the theme of Proverbs 8: *The gracious invitation of wisdom, more desirable than anything, existing before everything, is an invitation to fullness of life.* Only a fool would not heed the invitation of wisdom! But fools abound and the wise are few.

Wisdom Raises Her Voice

Let's look at the whole of the chapter before we center on its heart. Chapter 8 begins in this way: *Wisdom calls to all in gracious invitation to heed her instruction* (vv. 1-8).

> Does not wisdom call out?
> Does not understanding raise her voice? (v. 1).

The call of Lady Wisdom is not to the elite nor to those in ivory towers. In the Bible wisdom is not esoteric and is certainly not Gnostic. Wisdom is for everyone. Wisdom comes to the places where people live and work, and she calls out to them earnestly:

> "To you, O men, I call out;
> I raise my voice to all mankind" (v. 4).

Wisdom speaks only the truth, and her gifts are altogether good. In fact, her instruction is more precious than silver and her knowledge is more valuable than precious stones: "nothing you desire can compare with her" (v. 11).

Wisdom Exalts Herself
The second section of the paean to wisdom presents the exaltation of Lady Wisdom: *Wisdom exalts herself above all things describable and promises reward to those who heed her* (vv. 12-21). She associates herself with prudence, knowledge, and discretion and centers herself in the fear of Yahweh:

> By me kings reign
> and rulers make laws that are just;
> by me princes govern,
> and all nobles who rule on earth (vv. 15-16).

Wisdom describes herself as possessing riches and honor, fruit that is exquisite, and a righteous walk. Wisdom is beneficent to those who love her (v. 21).

Wisdom's Centerpiece
Yet it is in verses 22-31 that Lady Wisdom makes her most stunning claim: *Wisdom exists from the beginning of creation as a delight to God and finds her delight in men.* It is here that we find our centerpiece, to which we will return shortly. But first let's complete the chapter.

Wisdom's Final Offer

Following her audacious claim, Lady Wisdom then makes her final offer: *Wisdom offers the blessing of life to those who heed her but the cursing of death to those who reject her* (vv. 32-36). These overt warnings have precedents in the earlier chapters of Proverbs, but they are never so gripping as here. After displaying the reality of the issue, based upon her close association with God and her long history with man, Wisdom the Lady speaks in beatitude to the wise but in contempt to the fool:

> "Blessed is the man who listens to me,
>> watching daily at my doors,
>> waiting at my doorway.
> For whoever finds me finds life
>> and receives favor from the LORD.
> But whoever fails to find me harms himself;
>> all who hate me love death" (vv. 34-36).

In the Beginning

With this flow of the text now before us, we return to the pinnacle of our high text, verses 22-31. It is in this section that Lady Wisdom makes claims for herself that seem nearly incredible to us. She says that she has existed beside Yahweh from the very beginning of his work in creating the universe. Then she speaks of herself as a co-craftsperson, the special object of his joy. Listen to her words:

> "The LORD possessed me at the beginning of his work,
>> before his deeds of old;
> I was appointed from eternity,
>> from the beginning, before the world began.
> When there were no oceans, I was given birth,
>> when there were no springs abounding with water;
> before the mountains were settled in place,
>> before the hills, I was given birth" (vv. 22-25).[5]

Lady Wisdom was an attendant with God at the very beginning of creation. When Yahweh set the heavens in their place and the deep in its place, there she was. Whether it was clouds above or seas below, Wisdom is able to say, "I was there" (vv. 25-29). Constantly at his side, Lady Wisdom is rightly and beautifully pictured by Michelangelo nestled in the arm of the great creator Yahweh.

The last two verses of the section are the most mysterious and wonderful:

> "Then I was the craftsman[6] at his side.
> I was filled with delight day after day,
>   rejoicing always in his presence,
> rejoicing in his whole world
>   and delighting in mankind" (vv. 30-31).

Wisdom is given a great and joyful role in her association with God in his wonder-work of creation.[7]

Levels of Meaning

Yet what are we to make of this? Who or what is this important entity Wisdom?

I believe that in this intensely literary text, we may see three levels of meaning in the Hebrew term *hokmah*, "wisdom." When I speak here of "levels of meaning," I do not have in mind the medieval concepts that tended to obscure Scripture rather than to clarify it. I am thinking instead in a literary manner. Just as the reader of Melville's *Moby Dick* must see in the Great Whale more than just a large mammal, so in Wisdom *(hokmah)* we have more than the obvious.

As we study the use of wisdom *(hokmah)* in the wisdom literature of the Bible we find that one of the principal issues is that wisdom *(hokmah)* is the order that Yahweh has imposed on creation. It is this order that calls attention to itself as being desirable and as that which informs creation as being "good, yes, very good." This, of course, is a major contribution of the theology of creation in Genesis 1.

A second factor in our understanding of wisdom *(hokmah)* is that it clearly is something that existed prior to creation.[8] Wisdom *(hokmah)* was before God had done anything else; it is the first of the creations/possessions of Yahweh. It was from of old, from the beginning, when there were no mountains, before there were hills, before Yahweh had done anything that he has done—wisdom was his!

Wisdom does not come from the cosmos nor is it dependent on the cosmos. Wisdom is from Yahweh. Furthermore, wisdom *(ḥokmah)* is a demonstration of one of God's attributes. That is, it is part of the process of glorifying or manifesting God. As Psalm 19:1 begins, "the created cosmos manifests God's glory," so wisdom is the order in the universe that manifests the very attribute of God that is wisdom. This factor is heard in the singing of the seraphs in Isaiah 6:3: "the fullness of the whole earth is his glory" (personal translation).

Something of Himself

God has placed into the created order something of his glory, something of his wonder, something of himself. God is never to be confused with the world he has made. The Bible is distinct among all religious texts from the ancient (and modern) world; Yahweh is never identified with or confused in his creation. Nevertheless, creation shows the whorls of the divine fingerprint. When we look closely at what God has made, we may say—even shout—he has been there! This is a path where God has walked—see the prints of his feet. Here God has worked—see the wonders of his hand. The world is filled with wonder. I am wonder. All that God has touched is WONDER. Remember our study of the verb of creation, *bara'*? It is *wonder* that God has made; he makes it wherever he goes.

Once we have seen that wisdom is something God has put into the universe and that wisdom is something that is a part of God himself, then we are ready to assert that wisdom *(ḥokmah)* points forward to Christ. Here we may not speak of prophecy, for the language of Proverbs 8 is not prophetic. We also dare not speak of typology here, for when we speak of a type we need to speak of an antitype that exhausts the meaning of the type and makes the type unnecessary. For example, we may well regard sacrifice in the Old Testament period as types of the sacrifice of the Lord Jesus in his death on the cross. When we argue this way, we say that the sacrifices in the Old Testament were only meaningful because of the death of Christ, their true antitype; further, to continue to offer sacrifices in the Old Testament manner would be to bring contempt on the finality and reality of the death of Christ. When the antitype has come, the types are of value no longer, except as prior pointers to new realities. But this is not the case with wisdom.

Inner-Connections

I know of only one concept that helps me understand how wisdom (*ḥokmah*) relates to the Person of Christ in Proverbs 8. Unfortunately for you, my reader, the term that best describes this phenomenon is the long German polysyllable *Heilsgeschichte*. By this word I refer to the inner-connectedness of sacred history, where terms and concepts in the Old Testament that are not really types or prophecies still have an actual relationship to earlier or later issues, particularly culminating in the Person of the Savior Jesus.

The Divine Name

Let me illustrate this concept in the case of the name of God, Yahweh. In Exodus 3:14-15, God reveals his majestic name to Moses as he commissions his prophet for the work of leading Israel from the hand of Pharaoh. The issue is complex, but the name of God is a name that speaks of the glory of his Person and his grace to his people. By his name Yahweh, the Lord presented the realities of his self-existence and the relatedness he bears with his people. By his name, God asserted that he is the eternal one who is dependent upon none other for his being; yet he is the covenant one who will relate himself to his people forever. There is no greater mark of the grace of God in all of Scripture, save in the Incarnation, than there is in his name.

When we read certain New Testament texts in which the name of Jesus is tied to the name of Yahweh in the Old Testament, we come to the conclusion that in the Person of the Savior, the name of God is made more clear than ever (see John 1:18 for this function of the Savior). That Jesus was come to deliver his people from their sin (Matthew 1:21), is a basic property of the name Yahweh (see Exodus 3:8). That Jesus is the one who is able to say of himself, "I AM" (John 8:58) is a staggering identification with the basic concept of the name of God in the first revelation to Moses (Exodus 3:14)—and the strongest possible assertion by the Lord to his Jewish hearers that he was—and is—Yahweh in flesh! When Jesus said to his disciples that he would be with them until the close of the age (Matthew 28:20), he was building upon a basic meaning of the name Yahweh (see Exodus 3:12).

For these reasons we are able to speak of the name Jesus and the name Yahweh in the same breath: The name Jesus is the explication of the name Yahweh. But here is neither prophecy nor type. Exodus 3 is not a prophecy of a future revelation of the name of God; it *is* the revelation. Nevertheless, in the name Jesus the revelation is advanced and there is a continuity in that very revelation. Exodus 3 is not a type of the name of Jesus either. If it were a type, then the name Yahweh would be nullified by the name Jesus, as sacrifice is nullified by his death. Yet the biblical point of the name of God is that it is eternal—the very name speaks eternity: I AM.

So we come back to our ungainly German term *Heilsgeschichte*. (I have a friend who is a former secretary who still shudders at the thought of this word.) Until another is presented, this is the most serviceable word we have for a notable feature of the organic unity of the Scriptures. There is an inner-connectedness in revelation that is alongside the lines of prophetic and typological continuity that we have learned to expect.[9]

Wisdom and Christ

And so we return to wisdom (*ḥokmah*) in the lovely hymn of Proverbs 8. *Ultimately this term speaks of Christ*. The Arian error of centuries ago was in making an immediate connection. If wisdom *is* Christ, then Christ is less than God. But if wisdom *speaks of Christ* in the inner-connectedness of sacred history, then we see why it is that Paul describes Jesus Christ as he does in Colossians.

Surely Paul's words in Colossians 1:15-17 are built on the concepts of Proverbs 8:22-31. Read these words slowly, and sense how artistically and creatively the apostle Paul uses the language of the wisdom poem:

He is the image of the invisible God, the firstborn over all creation. For by him all things were created: things in heaven and on earth, visible and invisible, whether thrones or powers or rulers or authorities; all things were created by him and for him. He is before all things, and in him all things hold together.

Is it not on the basis of Proverbs 8 that the Gospel of John is able to say with the apostle Paul that Jesus is the co-creator with the Father of all that exists? "Through him all things were made; without him nothing was made that has been made" (John 1:3).

Further, in Colossians 2:3, the apostle says of Christ: "in whom are hidden all the treasures of wisdom and knowledge." These words mean that wisdom (*hokmah*) finds its ultimate expression in the Person of the Lord Jesus Christ. He is Wisdom Incarnate. Lady Wisdom, nestled in the arm of the Father in Proverbs 8, is Jesus the Son in Colossians 2. Our traditional categories of the offices of Christ turn out to be too limited. In addition to the standard offices of prophet, priest, and king, we need to add the office of sage. As Jesus is Prophet who surpasses Moses, Priest who excels Aaron, and King who exceeds David—so he is Sage who is wiser than Solomon. It is he who was with the Father, at his side, bringing joy and art and delight to the creative acts.

Moreover, any case for theological male chauvinism must come to an inglorious end in our observation that it is Lady Wisdom that speaks of Christ the Man.

Wisdom is the feminine vehicle of spirituality through which Yahweh bestows his presence and its benefits. . . . Man is pressed to welcome a reality which responds to his embrace because this reality initiates it. The analogy of love between woman and man rather than between man and woman corrects the implication of "male chauvinism," for it makes woman preeminent.[10]

Wonder, Attribute, and Savior

All of this is to say that in Proverbs 8 we have a three-level understanding of wisdom *(ḥokmah)*. Wisdom is the wonder and order that God has put into the cosmos. This fact is the basis for God's call for believers to enjoy science (which we shall stress in chapter 11). Wisdom is further an attribute of God, singled out from him for particular display. Now watch this: The attribute of wisdom which is of God becomes an attribute of the world that he has made. In some mysterious sense, "this world order turns, as a person, towards men, wooing them and encouraging them in direct address."[11] Finally wisdom points forward to God's wisdom in Jesus Christ. We are able to remain within a sound interpretive procedure in Proverbs 8, and yet see the continuity that leads to the Person of Jesus—which the New Testament demands.

> In Proverbs 8:1-35 Wisdom seems to incorporate a divine self-claim that antedates the creation, somehow stands in relationship to the one God (8:22-31), and assists in the creation of the world and man. Wisdom in Proverbs 8 . . . is at once the order that God has imposed upon creation, is "from God" and prior to creation (8:22), and points forward to Christ (8:32-36, cf. John 1:3; Col. 1:16-18; 2:3). Wisdom is God's associate in whom God delights. Wisdom has a distinctive existence in God's presence and is somehow distinctively related to the created world.[12]

Listen to Her Laugh!

And how is Lady Wisdom/Jesus the Sage related to the created world? In joy!

Wisdom laughs as she sees what God is doing. Wisdom laughs as she joins him in his creative tasks. And Wisdom's most joyful laugh is with man, in whom she has abundant delight:

"I was the craftsman at his side.
I was filled with delight day after day,
    rejoicing always in his presence,
rejoicing in his whole world
    and delighting in mankind" (Proverbs 8:30-31).

Often our view of the Lord Jesus is a view of one who is mournful, grieving, sad. When the Savior came to do his work of salvation, he was not recognized by the world he had made and was rejected by his own for whom he came (John 1:10-11). In his suffering he lost beauty and majesty,

He was despised and rejected by men,
    a man of sorrows, and familiar with suffering.
                              (Isaiah 53:3)

But in creation he laughed! In the making of man he delighted! It is in fact that exuberance of laughter in Proverbs 8:30-31 that has led some writers to think that the term "craftsman" should be translated "child." But there Wisdom is. The Lady laughs with God and man. *There Christ is!* It is his laughter we hear as we learn to be human in wisdom.

Another Laugh

But there is another laughter that we face if we choose folly rather than wisdom; this is Wisdom's laughter of scorn. This laugh, not unlike that of God in heaven against his foes in the great and coming battle of Armageddon (see Psalm 2:4), is a laugh of judgment:

"But since you rejected me when I called
    and no one gave heed when I stretched out my
hand,
since you ignored all my advice
    and would not accept my rebuke,
I in turn will laugh at your disaster;
    I will mock when calamity overtakes you."
                              (Proverbs 1:24-26)

Terrien writes:

Wisdom danced and played *(saḥeq)* in the presence
of Yahweh at the birth of the world. Wisdom will
now laugh *(saḥaq)* at those who use their "free will"
in order to divorce themselves from "knowledge"
and "the fear of Yahweh."[13]

With His Arm about Wisdom

When God made man as male and female, his arm was en-
circling wisdom. Wisdom laughed at the creation of man—a
laugh of joy and delight. As we think back to the ceiling fresco
of the great Michelangelo, we now observe that he has painted
her too somber, too anxious. He has Lady Wisdom looking too
far ahead at the moment of the touch of the finger of man by the
finger of God. At that moment, Wisdom was laughing!

You and I are called upon by Lady Wisdom—even Jesus
the Sage—to live lives of genuine humanity as a celebration of
the laugh of Wisdom at our making. (In the next chapter we
shall see some ways in which this may be done.)

As we live for the glory of God in a world far too filled with
pain and suffering, let us hear the laughter again! Let us learn
with Eric Liddell (as expressed in his wonderful line in the film,
Chariots of Fire) that when we run we may sense God's smile
upon us!

Let us be truly human in God's wisdom.

Chapter 10, Notes

1. Charles H. Morgan, *The Life of Michelangelo* (New York: Reynal &
Co., 1960), 90.

2. Ibid., 99.

3. See Samuel Terrien, *The Elusive Presence: Toward a New Biblical
Theology*, vol. 26 of *Religious Perspectives*, ed. Ruth Nanda Anshen (San
Francisco: Harper & Row, 1978), 350-89. Among those who see the figure of
the woman as Eve is Kenneth Clark in *Civilisation: A Personal View* (New
York: Harper & Row, 1970), 129.

4. A sampling of African proverbs is given by James and Jeanette Krabill, "To Put It in Other Words," *Festival Quarterly* (May-July, 1983), 30. I find it fascinating to ask missionaries who work with tribal peoples to tell me some of the proverbs that are used by the people in their areas.

5. The NIV which I have quoted here expresses the issues well, but there are factors in these words that are matters of an ancient, and continuing, debate. The words of verse 22, "the LORD possessed me," could be translated "the LORD created me." In fact, this possible confusion has led to serious problems among those who have anticipated that wisdom and Christ are to be identified in this passage. A premature judgment on this text figured prominently in the Arian-Athanasian controversy, and is reflected in the Nicene Creed in the words, "begotten, not made." Those who have made that identification have laid themselves open to the possibility that Christ had a beginning sometime before the universe. It would not matter how far one would push that beginning back; if Christ did in fact have a beginning, then he is less truly deity than is the Father. We need to walk very carefully in the pathway of this text. Further, even if the words of verse 22 are agreed to be noncommittal concerning beginnings, verses 24 and 25 speak of the birth (begetting) of wisdom in the context of original creation, and not Incarnation.

6. The Hebrew term translated "craftsman" is particularly problematic, as may be demonstrated by the reading of standard commentaries on this text (a common alternative is "little child"). For our purposes we do not need to solve these problems at this point.

7. See Gerhard von Rad, *Wisdom in Israel* (Nashville: Abingdon Press, 1972), 144-76. This section is extremely important in the study of the nature of wisdom in Proverbs 8.

8. This is true regardless of how we translate the disputed word of verse 22 (*qanani:* "Yahweh created me" or "Yahweh possessed me"). In either translation, the act involved preceded the making of the heavens and the earth.

9. I have developed these ideas in a paper presented to the Evangelical Theological Society, "Is There *Heil* for *Heilsgeschichte*?" (presented at the Reformed Theological Seminary, Jackson, Miss., December 1975). In this paper I sought to recapture the term from liberal scholarship. J. K. C. von Hofmann, whose name is associated with the early use of this term, did not use it to divorce the facts of history from the preaching of the story, as is so common in the usual use of this term in our own day. See also Gerhard Hasel, *Old Testament Theology: Basic Issues in the Current Debate* (Grand Rapids: Wm. B. Eerdmans Publishing Co., 1972), 77-78.

10. Terrien, *The Elusive Presence*, 358.

11. Von Rad, *Wisdom in Israel*, 156.

12. In this section from *God, Revelation and Authority*, Carl F. H. Henry paraphrases a lecture I gave at Regent College in 1977. It is a little thing for me to quote Dr. Carl F. H. Henry. It is something else when he quotes me! See *God, Revelation and Authority*, 6 vols. (Waco, Tex.: Word Books, 1979), 3:320.

13. Terrien, *The Elusive Presence*, 380.

Thersites: *Lechery, lechery; still wars and lechery; nothing else holds fashion: a burning devil take them!*
Shakespeare
Troilus and Cressida

Finally, brothers, whatever is true, whatever is noble, whatever is right, whatever is pure, whatever is lovely, whatever is admirable—if anything is excellent or praiseworthy—think about such things.
The Apostle Paul

In a Christian framework all truth is God's truth and all beauty God's beauty. And discovery about the truth or beauty of literature is therefore a contribution toward the cultural mandate of subduing God's world for his glory.
Leland Ryken
Triumphs of the Imagination

Chapter 11

Being Human in the World

*O*ne might have thought that Shakespeare's character Thersites, that "deformed and scurrilous Grecian," was writing today when he speaks of lechery and war as the only things in fashion. Perhaps he had spent a day watching soap operas (now both daytime and nighttime on American television—surely an overflowing cup!). And the words of Paul about the good and the pure—where may such be found in our decadent day? If John White is correct that the real problem with the church today is one of worldliness,[1] how may Leland Ryken pretend to find that which is ennobling in worldly literature? How may we live as truly human in our wicked age?

Know Nothing But Christ

In my years of teaching at the seminary I have come to know a great variety of students. From time to time I come across the modern monastic, or at least as near to a monastic as can be found in a Baptist school. I remember one fine student who told me that he did not subscribe to any newspapers or newsmagazines. He did not watch television. He did not even own a radio. The only books he would read outside of the Bible were books written by Christian authors, and then only if he had

173

them on good recommendations from trusted Christian friends. To him sporting events, world politics, the daily funnies, and consumer ads were against "knowing Christ and him crucified." His reasons were based on a fear of distraction from the gospel and a desire to maintain a pure mind, a mind undefiled with the pollutants of the world.

It is difficult to condemn such a student. Would that his single-mindedness toward Christ and the things of God was more evident in more of our students! I suppose some students—and even some of their teachers—spend more time with the daily paper than with their Bibles. Moreover, this type of student is echoing an ancient Christian sentiment that was first stated by Tertullian, who asked, "What indeed has Athens to do with Jerusalem? What concord is there between the Academy and the Church? What between heretics and Christians?"[2]

Nevertheless, I cannot commend such an attitude. One does not have to be a reformed drunkard to speak against the ills of booze, but I do believe that the Christian youth worker (to take one example) has to be sufficiently aware of the culture of his day that he at least is acquainted with Pac-Man.

Even with his strong charge against worldliness, White admits the need for an awareness of our surrounding culture:

> I suppose what are needed are men and women of God, in touch with both the contemporary culture and the Spirit of God, who will explain and teach those undealt-with sections of the Scripture so specially needed by the people of God."[3]

It is possible—in fact it is imperative—that the Christian humanist know his culture well, but that his approach to life continue to be single-minded devotion to Christ. The learned Christian apologist Cornelius Van Til was never a stranger to the world about him, but he determined to bring all knowledge captive to the obedience of Christ. He did not shut himself off from the world; he sought to understand it in relationship to the Person of Christ as the Creator-Redeemer of himself and of his world. He states, "All my life, my life in my family, my life in my church, my life in society, and my life in my vocation as a minister of the gospel and a teacher of Christian apologetics is unified under the banner *Pro Rege* [for the King]!"[4]

Jews and Christians in Dialogue

Recently I was in a public forum, a dialogue on Jewish and Christian views of the kingdom of God. My learned friend, a rabbi in our community, spoke eloquently on the contemporary Jewish view that man is innately good and that it is the responsibility of man to improve this world and to achieve with God the realization of the kingdom of God on earth. He then spoke of his view of the widespread Christian ideal of the abdication of hope for the kingdom of God on this earth, with its other-worldliness and its pessimism concerning this world and the things of this world.

As I listened to my friend, I desired not to intensify the debate but to put it in balance. I desired to state that some Christians believe in both the kingdom of God on earth as well as the hope of heaven, but that both will be achieved not by the labor of man but by the irruption of God into human affairs.

But I wished as well to ask why it is that so many Christians have such an unbalanced view of this world and their place in it. We do not believe in the innate goodness of man, of course; we believe that man is very fallen. But does our doctrine of the fallenness of man mean that we are not to be concerned with the ailing and the hurting of the world? How many times will we hear preachers say that to be involved in social betterment is merely "rearranging the deck chairs on the Titanic"? Where is the historic evangelical concern for the needs of hurting people and for improving their lot in this world?

It is true that we are pilgrims, that we are in the world and not of it, that our home is in heaven and our heart ought to be on the things of heaven and not of earth. It is also true (as John White strongly chides) that the church behaves at times as though it is shacked up with the world, even though it is engaged to the Lord Jesus Christ.[5]

Yet the Christian is not to be so out of the world that he is of no good to the world. Nor is the Christian to be so out of the world that he ceases to see the good that is in it. If we have understood the concept of biblical wisdom rightly, the believer may find the whorls of the divine fingerprint in many unexpected places. But we must learn how to look and how to respond.

Lechery and Loveliness

In a world filled with "lechery and war" there is also that which is "true, noble, right, pure, lovely, admirable, excellent and praiseworthy." We are commanded to think about such things and to learn from them. This is a central part of being truly human. In this chapter we shall make some suggestions on how to live in this manner as we consider self, creation, things, and others. In all things, our model is the Lord Jesus Christ who has recaptured for us what it means to live this side of Eden as one who is truly human.

Living with Self

In each of the areas of our living we find that which is negative and that which is positive. It is not difficult to come up with a litany of evil concerning the self. From my youth I remember the words of weekly congregational confession of sin: "Almighty God, we confess unto Thee that we are by nature sinful and unclean, and that we have sinned against Thee by thought, word and deed." An argument can be made, I suppose, that those who say such words week in and week out may cease to think seriously of them (yet when we generalize here, we are in danger of a considerable slur against fellow believers). But an argument may also be made that those in churches where no weekly confession of sin is made are not likely to think of the reality of sin in their lives either.

It is not difficult to think of negative elements we all face in coping with the self. Yet we must learn to assert the positive elements as well, for in the doctrine of the Incarnation of the Savior we find a new dignity for the self related in righteousness to God.

Devotions Where?

Have you come to grips with the implications of the Incarnation upon your own view of your body? Whereas the flesh may be a source of sin and a provocateur of rebellion against God, the body itself is God's gift of wonder.

I respond to the writer Madeleine L'Engle in somewhat the same way I respond to Frederick Buechner. They both say things that are a bit off-center, but they say them so well! In one of her recent books, L'Engle tells of an encounter she had with a young man who was being examined for the Episcopal priesthood. One of her questions to the young man concerned his habits of prayer. When he said that he did not have time to read the morning prayer because of business, L'Engle said to him, "All it takes is ten minutes! Why don't you read it on the john?" She then reports:

> To my amazement, I had shocked him. He asked, "But isn't that sacrilegious?"
>
> Almost equally shocked by this response, I said, "That is a very unincarnational question."
>
> One of my priest friends reminded him that Luther had done some deep theological thinking on what, in his day, was called the jakes, and all three of us tried to get over to him that life cannot be separated into secular and sacred, that if God created everything, and called it good, then all of life is good, and only we can see it as sacrilegious. There is nothing which is, of itself, sacrilegious. Just as the act of making love can be sacramental, so can all aspects of our lives, even the most lowly. If we cannot pray in the bathroom, it is not likely that we will be able to pray anywhere.[6]

Do you find yourself uncomfortable with L'Engle's point of view? Perhaps it would help to hear it from "the theologian's theologian," the late Dr. John Murray of Westminster Seminary:

The highest reaches of true spirituality are dependent upon events that occurred in the realm of the physical and sensuous. A religion that can be indifferent to the bodily, to the physical, to the phenomenal, has no affinity with the Christian faith; it is a spurious religiosity that does not warrant the name 'spirituality.'[7]

Male Weepies

Not only does the believer have to come to grips with the fact of his or her body as a good creation of God, an essential and holy part of the wonder of one's being; the true believer also has to come to grips with his or her emotions. This is particularly true of the male believer, I suspect.

Syndicated columnist Russell Baker describes the movie *Chariots of Fire* as a "male weepie." By this he means that the film worked because it allowed a man to have a lump in the throat, but did not demand that he sob out loud. He says that men like to cry as well as women, but do not like to cry out loud. A "male weepie" is a movie that gives a comfortable, nonembarrassing lump in the throat, but no tears on the cheek.[8]

I understand what Baker is saying, and I laugh at the clever insight he has. I am sure that he is correct in his understanding of male foibles. I have enjoyed *M*A*S*H*, for example, not just for its zany comedy (was there ever a better noun than *M*A*S*H* for the adjective "zany"?), but for its gentle touch of common humanity, particularly in scenes of Colonel Sherman Potter with his lump in the throat. But I also know that the Paragon of adult masculine humanity was not only able to have a lump in his throat; he was able to weep out loud without embarrassment. The words "Jesus wept" (John 11:35) do not call for sniveling men constantly grasping for tissues. But these words do allow a man to weep when the occasion demands weeping. I recall an occasion where a roomful of adult Christian men were openly weeping because of the confession of sin by one of their number. In that moment of shared humanity, the tears of these men flowed with the tears of the Savior, and his humanity became our own. "Male weepie" indeed!

In Touch with Feelings

One Easter Sunday morning began with a personal sadness on our little farmlet. One of our dairy goats, a beautiful young doe, had somehow gotten her neck caught in the vertical bars of the manger during the night. She must have panicked. In her struggle she brought the heavy manger down to the floor, and in the process had broken her neck.

When I found her lying on the floor of the barn early that morning, she was barely strong enough to whimper. I knew that nothing could be done to save her and that on that early Sunday morning, before we could go to church, I would have to dispatch her—something I had never done with a goat before.

I have a six-foot shelf of books on being a "gentleman farmer," for, as a city boy, everything on the farm is new to me. I took a moment to read from *Country Women,* a book written as a part of the feminist movement in the sixties and directed to that portion of the women's movement that was moving to the farm. The reason I read from this book was that it not only gave me a series of step-by-step instructions and photos on how to butcher my goat, it also told me how I would feel when I did it and how to come to grips with those feelings. (The books written by men do not mention much about feelings in butchering—just where to cut.)

But even this sensitively written book did not present fully the feelings I had that morning. That morning was Easter! I had led in Passover *seders* over the last two nights and had spoken of the sacrifice of lamb (and goat!) that Passover presents as a picture of the death of the Savior Jesus. This may sound trite to you, even silly; but I do not know of an Easter season that I felt so deeply the death my Savior died as that morning when I had to kill my beautiful doe.

The Shorthand of Emotion

One of the most wonderful ways to get in touch with one's emotions is by means of music, which Tolstoy called "the shorthand of emotion." Think what music means to you in your Christian life. Then think how impoverished your Christian life would be without it. It is no accident that the largest book of the

Bible is a book of music. It is also providential that the musical settings of the Psalms have not been preserved, so that the art of music might develop and flourish through time.[9]

There are some hymns that I have associated so strongly with certain events in my life that, like the vivid memory prompted by a certain smell, I am able to recall the emotions of that moment with intensity and clarity. Even as I type these words I find that I am nearly overcome as I think of the hymn, "It Is Well with My Soul," and the time that my friend John Adams sang these lines just before I was to preach a sermon in our church, and all the while our daughter was in critical condition in the hospital. The words of the hymn bring it all back, and I am deeply moved.

But I am moved not just by hymns and praise songs. I am moved by great music of all kinds. I sense my humanity more keenly in music than in nearly any other human activity.

From the Back Row

Douglas Yeo has the right attitude about music. He is bass trombonist for the Baltimore Symphony Orchestra. In an article in *Christianity Today* he describes what it is to make music from the back row of the orchestra. He says that his back row seat is the best seat in the house, except for that of the conductor. He is able to hear every note, see every movement, and have a heightened awareness of the music. Yeo then speaks of musicianship and Christian faith:

> When a Christian makes music he is not merely participating in the scientific phenomena of vibrating columns of air to produce what we know as music. Music making is an intense spiritual experience, a celebration of creation, an act of love. And when the audience responds with a thunderous ovation, it is not the members of the orchestra, or Beethoven, or Wagner, or Copland they are applauding, but, whether they know it or not, it is the living God. It is God alone who bestows on composers the mysteri-

ous gift of composition, and on performers that unspeakable gift of interpretation. [10]

This is thinking Christianly about music. This is allowing
music to help one respond as truly human to the Giver of Song.
Yeo says that he and fellow trombonist Eric Carlson, also a
Christian musician, find that when the music is done well, "we
get a glimpse of the Garden of Eden; we experience an instant of
heaven." [11] That's it!

What a wonderful expression of shared humanity music
may be! By music the Christian may sense Eden and heaven.
Through music the Christian performer and auditor join God in
one of his greatest gifts—and respond to him in wonder.

Human in Creation

We are well aware of the dangers of certain attitudes toward creation that bear on our behavior and life. The dogged
materialism of Carl Sagan, the cult of scientism, and the errors
of premature judgments—these are all well known. When
Sagan speaks of the cosmos as a new deity, as all there is or ever
was or ever will be, we are rightly shocked and we correctly turn
away.

But Christians should not fear nature nor the study of science. If anything, Christians should be on the forefront of the
ranks of those who love nature and search out its mysteries. For
when Sagan says that the study of science is our birthright, it is
we who must say a strong "Amen!"

The Christian and Science

A few years ago I was a guest professor at Regent College
in Vancouver, British Columbia. Among the other guests that
summer session was the British scholar Donald M. Mackay, a
noted brain scientist at the University of Keele in England. He
and Dr. R. Hooykaas of the Netherlands were teaching a course
together titled "Bible and Science." During one evening meal I
turned to Dr. Mackay, the author of such books as *The Clock
Work Image, Human Science & Human Dignity,* and *Brains,*

Machines and Persons, and I asked him to comment upon his course. I assumed that the course was on the evolution and creation debate.

Mackay told me in no uncertain terms that the course was not centered on the evolution-creation debate but was instead directed toward developing a positive attitude among Christian students toward science. I was intrigued by this disclosure and presumed to share an insight that had just come to me that week. My own course was on biblical theology, and I pointed out to Dr. Mackay a verse in the Psalms that I had presented in a lecture that day:

> Great are the works of the LORD;
>> they are pondered by all who delight in them.
>>> (Psalm 111:2)

As we discussed that text I remember his growing excitement. "That is it! That is it, precisely," he said, gesturing with knife and fork. Scripture does not present creation as a neutral factor, to be taken or ignored as one wills. Scripture presents the creation of God as compelling attention from the people of faith. Scientific research was long associated with monks as a part of their holy work. It is high time that Christians again see scientific research as a high and holy calling leading to worship of the Creator of all things by his people.

The Christian in Medical Studies

Recently I shared these thoughts in a devotional talk to a fellowship of Christian medical and dental students at the state medical school in our city. I was amazed at the responses I got. Some told me of the guilt they had been feeling because they were studying science and not Bible. I encouraged them not to neglect their Bibles, but also to see in their study of science all manner of opportunities to give praise to God for the wonders he has made and to which he has called us to find delight. Just as they learned to pray before reading their Bible to learn of the things of God, I encouraged them to pray before opening their books on anatomy or chemistry, for in these books they would be learning the things of God as well. This is true whether the authors of those books were aware or not of the reality of God in the subject matters under discussion. The Christian may pray for wisdom as he studies biology in the same way he prays for wisdom in the reading of the gospel, if he has come to grips with the theology of wisdom in God's creation. Here the burden of the previous chapter becomes the reality of our living.

Not long after, I received a long distance phone call from a medical student at a major Eastern university. He had read an article I had written on nakedness in the Bible[12] which had led him to serious soul-searching concerning the propriety of his medical studies. How, he wondered, could a medical student look upon a naked body and not be guilty of the sins described in Leviticus 18? I tried to explain to him that the expression, "to uncover the nakedness of," (KJV) found throughout that chapter, speaks of the intention of sexual relations (as in the NIV). He was afraid that the Bible stood against him in his study of the human body and the alleviation of disease and pain. No! There is no area of legitimate scientific research that is forbidden the believer. Only research that is clearly based on perversions or deliberate acts of dehumanization is forbidden. For the rest, there is the gift of God: explore, learn, triumph—and praise God for the task! It is a task He gives only to us. The angels have no beatitude from Yahweh on the study of nature; this is a blessing only for man as male and female.

The Christian and Nature

Nature is ours to enjoy! The wilderness is for our exultation in the wonder of Yahweh. We are misled if we allow the enthusiasm of nontheistic naturalists to steal our thunder. Philip Yancey asks why Christian novelists do not make more of nature. This is our realm, because we know the Creator to whom it belongs. "The concept of creation is, at heart, a Christian concept."[13]

> The earth is the LORD's, and everything in it,
>   the world, and all who live in it (Psalm 24:1).

It is this world that God turns over to the man and woman who reflect his glory and majesty, and he tells them to subdue it and to rule it and to experience his wonder in it. Christians dare not leave nature to nontheistic naturalists, nor ecology to neopantheists, nor science to sub-Christian religionists.

The Great Elk Hunt

To say that I am not an award-winning bow hunter is an overstatement. In two week-long hunts I have yet to bring home an animal. I have yet to hit an animal. I have hardly let an arrow fly. In fact, after last year's hunt I may not be able to go back to the woods at all, at least not with the same hunting buddies. Oh, what shame!

I was given a shot opportunity rarely seen by bow hunters—the kind hunters dream about on those cold rainy nights around the fire. It was the type of shot that I would never dare request from God—it was too much. But I suffered a fatal moment of buck fever, and the animal got by. I shot after the moment had passed. (As I sat there on the log, finishing my apple, swallowing my pride, I felt raindrops on my head. But I had seen no clouds; the sky was blue. The drops must have been the tears of angels who flew away saying this was the last chance for Allen!)

But the point of the hunt was still realized. This is what I told my family as I came home meatless again. When a group of Christian men go into a primitive wilderness area for a week to hunt with bow and arrow, they are going on a pilgrimage. They have time to talk together in camp as never in town. And they have time to commune with God alone in the woods in a way rarely experienced in the office. Hang the elk! I had been in the wilderness and was by that fact drawn close to God. The angels may have fled, but God was truly near. Let's not leave the woods only to beer-drinking men who may be better hunters but who are unaware of greater realities.

A Chary Caution

When we think of nature as God's world, our perspective is truly different from those who share the same space. For these reasons, let's continue to be chary of premature statements by nonbelieving theorists. When Russian cosmonaut Yuri Gagarin said in 1961 that he had traveled around the earth and had not seen God, it was—as Dr. W. A. Criswell said—a premature decision.

But let us at the same time stop fearing science. The study of God's creation may be as sacred a task as any ministry can be. I have friends who are research chemists with a major Eastern chemical concern. Dr. Marina Adamich Saltman tells me that when she and her husband Robert enter their scientific laboratories, it is with humble and determined prayer to God that their work that day would bring blessing to man and praise to God. She says that every day is a day of potential discovery of something new about the wonder of nature and of God's created order. This is an attitude of wonder that makes a believer truly human in the context of God's creation.

Before we leave the subject of nature and the Creator, jot down a task for personal Bible study. Read the Book of Isaiah sometime asking one question: What uses does the prophet make of the natural world? I think you will be amazed in just a few chapters. Then turn to the Gospels. Read the records of the life of Christ on earth, again asking the same question. Look at how prominent elements of nature and the created world are in his teaching and in his wonder-works. Again, Jesus is our model.

Thinking Christianly about Things

Here is an area fraught with terrible danger. The minute we think we have things in their proper place in our lives, the ugly deity Mammon raises her wretched head in a new closet of our lives. This goddess is parthenogenetic; she is able to reproduce her kind at will, needing no paramour. She is also anaerobic; like certain bacteria, she is able to live and grow in places where there is no reason to suspect that she is alive. This goddess Mammon grows best in areas of total darkness, for she knows nothing at all of light. Then, when we least expect it, she bursts from the hidden closets of our lives in a new and deadly mutation.

Think, for example, of the encouragements given to Christian people to give to worthy causes—a Christian grace. But that grace may be exploited and manipulated by greedy men as, for example, some electronic hucksters of religion who plead for yet another twenty-dollar gift in exchange for a five-and-ten bauble, the Protestant equivalent of medieval popery at its worst.

We do not speak in condemnation of all. Of course not! But there are those who condemn themselves. Widows on Social Security are seen as sheep to be fleeced to support the extravagant and gaudy life-styles of these religionists. Film aficionados who lament the death of the old Hollywood have only to look to the Sunday morning television ghetto to see where the new Hollywood may be found. Recent studies have shown that these programs present pressing needs—survival needs—in excess of $180 per viewer-hour. And the homes worth $2.5 million and up, the clothing and jewels, the Lear jets, the northwoods properties—do these not call to mind the words of Amos:

> You lie on beds inlaid with ivory
>   and lounge on your couches.
> You dine on choice lambs
>   and fattened calves (Amos 6:4)?

But the moment I blast at another's materialism, that old bestial goddess Mammon smirks as she breeds in my own closet. When I preach on the true worship of God, are my thoughts and desires pure and unstained? How much do I think of the book table in the narthex and wonder if my preaching will lead some to buy my books? "Oh, but they need my books to follow more fully what I am stressing in the sermon." That's right, they do. And the fact that outrageous payments are due for my daughter's college tuition is not really a factor, is it? If you are near enough to hear it, Mammon's derisive laughter can be detected once again. (John White's book, *The Golden Cow*, is essential reading in this area for all of us. I have only one question of White: Does he have a book table when he speaks on these issues?)

I suspect that the only thing we may say of *things* is that the battle must continue or the battle will be lost. It is never things as *things*, but our *attitude* toward things that may destroy us—or liberate us. This is always true when we elevate things above persons.

A Common Concern

Materialism is not just a concern of Christians. It is an increasing concern even in the public media which so often tends to promote it. In one "Barney Miller" episode, a dapper police officer, Sergeant Harris, was working two jobs so that he could continue to buy fine wines and attend the opera. A fellow officer with more common tastes asked him what was wrong with beer and bowling. Harris responded, "That's not life; that's only gusto!"

Another example of secular concern for the materialism of our age is found in the Alan Alda film, *The Four Seasons*. At the end of the film is a scene of bittersweet humor. Jack Weston's character, Danny Zimmer, is rescued from drowning after he had fallen through thin ice into a frozen lake; but his prized Mercedes slips into the same lake that nearly took his life. All the way up the hill he alternates prayers of thanks to God for saving his life with curses to his friends for the loss of his car. And we laugh with him as we laugh at him, for we are cut from the same cloth. That goddess Mammon confuses us so, we have trouble being thankful even for our life.

Color or Black-and-White

Materialism comes in many forms. One is the false pride that sometimes comes in *not* making certain purchases. Remember in the 1960s when color television was coming into its own? In some pockets of evangelical Christianity it was all right for one to own a black-and-white set, but it was unspiritual to own a color set. One of my dear friends and seminary professors, an intensely spiritual man, owned up one day to owning a color set. When asked to justify this, Dr. Haddon Robinson said, "I prefer to watch television in color." He did not even use the traditional Christian escape clause, "but I found it on sale." Mammon slunk back a bit, but she is still around. We need to beat her back at all times.

Again, it is Jesus who is our model. Never possessed by things, he always placed people first. At his death he owned only his garment, and the soldiers gambled over that. Yet during his life he was equally comfortable in feasting with the very wealthy or fasting with the poor. We may presume as well that both the poor and the rich were comfortable with him. Jesus would be equally at home today in the inner-city tenement as he would in the country estate—and he would make the people comfortable in either place, so long as God is worshiped and not the harlot deity Mammon.

Thinking Christianly about Others

We mislead ourselves and betray our faith when we minimize the evil in man. It will not increase the dignity of man to pretend that he is basically good. This is a false dignity and is doomed to disappointment and ruin. I should never be shocked at the evil in another; I need only see in my own thoughts and works the ever-present seed of potential ruin.

But when I as a Christian humanist think of others, I must refuse to participate in indignities of any kind that will debase a fellow image-bearer of the God of creation. One of the great debasers of persons in our day is pornography. Some recent studies have shown direct connections between repeated exposures to pornography and sexual offenses. This comes as no surprise to the Christian, I suppose; but it was a surprise to some of the researchers who expected pornography to be neutral.[14] All other forms of sexual abuse and power ploys are to be fought as well. We as believers in the dignity of man cannot participate in indignities to man. Where we need help, let us get help. That too is a part of being human.

One in Christ

Further, Christians can have nothing more to do with racism, sexism, and anti-Semitism. There may have been a time when individual clusters of white Christians could be excused for these evils because of their upbringing and culture. But the time for that excuse has run out. Where is the strong preaching of the gospel message that racism has no place in Christian thinking? Listen again to the words of Paul: "There is neither Jew nor Greek, slave nor free, male nor female, for you are all one in Christ Jesus" (Galatians 3:28).

We need to eschew racism in all its forms, from the overt act to the covert thought. Ethnic jokes that have their humor only in the belittling of people on the basis of race or culture need to become no longer funny to us.

Moreover, we need to learn that racism cuts both ways. Many peoples of the world have a sense that they are "the people," and others are not quite on the same order. Many African tribal peoples, for example, have in their own languages the term "people" for themselves and "others" for the rest. Ethnocentricity is not a monopoly of WASP. Yet a shared sin is no excuse for sin. And we need to face this fact: To have low regard for any people on the basis of color, race, or national origin is to sin against the gospel of Christ in whom all men may become truly one, heirs together of the covenant of Abraham.

The Little Woman

Sexism is so common, even among godly people, that the expression of it often is not even recognized. Preachers who are highly spiritual and who have no desire to hurt anyone still tell stories on their wives about the dents in the fender and how much patience it takes to show their unconditional love. A woman professor at a leading Bible school started tabulating the number of times that this kind of story was told in chapel sermons by guest speakers. She gave up counting. Most, I am sure, were unaware of the offense they were causing.

Again, we need to turn to Jesus for our model for humanity. Against the twin evils of racism and sexism the Lord Jesus struck the final blow when he sat down at Jacob's well and spoke with the Samaritan woman not only about her own personal needs, but about the deepest areas of the theology of the worship of Yahweh (John 4).

Jesus and Women

Jesus never married. He was an itinerant preacher in the company of men. It would have been the expected thing for him to have avoided women altogether, except as they might come to him in crowds. But time after time in the years of his ministry, Jesus sought out the company of women. Time after time Jesus honored women. Time after time Jesus taught and encouraged and strengthened women. Against the grain of his culture, Christ the Tiger scratched out a whole new approach to understanding our humanity. We are man as male and female. Jesus, the single man in the company of men, needed also the company of women.

And it was the women who needed him. It was also the women who were most faithful to him. While the men with whom Jesus had spent the bulk of his time were in hiding, it was the women whom he had taught and whom he had honored who were at the foot of the cross, grieving at his dying. It was to a woman that he first displayed his glory in his resurrection body. In the life and ministry of Jesus we have the model for being truly human as male and female.

To All the World

We cannot relate better to others than as we bring them to the knowledge of the Savior Jesus and, with them, live this life in praise of God. The familiar words of the Great Commission, " ' All authority in heaven and on earth has been given to me' " (Matthew 28:18), suggest that Jesus, the new Adam, is reclaiming and enlarging the commission first given to Adam and Eve in the Garden of Eden. At that time our first parents were given authority by God to subdue the world for God's glory. To the extent that the sin of Adam caused him to lose that authority, the righteousness of Christ in his death and resurrection allows him to recapture that authority—and more besides. Whereas to first Adam was granted power over nature and animal life, to Christ is granted power over spiritual realities, to lead people to make disciples of all nations.[15]

This understanding suggests that world mission is the central focus of being truly human in Christ. Everything we have said in this chapter may come to rest here. The ultimate expression of shared dignity is the sharing of the gospel of Christ to others worldwide, in every culture, in every language. A genuine, biblical view of humanity in Christ simply will not let one rest at ease in Zion.

Lechery and the Lovely

Ours is a world of lechery and war. It is also a world of the good, the beautiful, and the lovely. Eschew lechery; embrace the lovely—and live for the praise of God in the only world we have!

Chapter 11, Notes

1. John White, *Flirting with the World: A Challenge to Loyalty* (Wheaton, Ill.: Harold Shaw, 1982).

2. The fascinating story of the quest for Christian scholarship in the legacy of Tertullian's charge is presented by E. Harris Harbison, *The Christian Scholar in the Age of Reformation* (1956; Grand Rapids: Wm. B. Eerdmans Publishing Co., 1983), especially chapter 1, "Scholarship as a Christian Calling," 1-29.

3. White, *Flirting with the World*, 131.

4. Cornelius Van Til, "My Credo," in *Jerusalem and Athens: Critical Discussions on the Theology and Apologetics of Cornelius Van Til*, ed. E. R. Geehan (Philadelphia: Presbyterian and Reformed Publishing Co., 1971), 5.

5. White, *Flirting with the World*, 9-13.

6. Madeleine L'Engle, *And It Was Good* (Wheaton, Ill.: Harold Shaw, 1983), 57.

7. John Murray, *Collected Writings*, vol. 2: *Select Lectures in Systematic Theology* (Edinburgh: The Banner of Truth Trust, 1977), 17.

8. Russell Baker, "The Male Weepie," in *The Rescue of Miss Yaskell, and Other Pipe Dreams* (New York: Congdon & Weed, 1983), 167.

9. This is a point that I have developed in an article on the Psalms and contemporary music. See "Put a New Psalm in Your Heart," *Moody Monthly*, April 1984, 37-38.

10. Douglas Yeo, "The View from the Back Row," *Christianity Today*, 21 January 1983, 40.

11. Ibid.

12. My article is in *The Theological Wordbook of the Old Testament*, 2 vols., ed. R. Laird Harris, Gleason L. Archer, Jr., and Bruce K. Waltke (Chicago: Moody Press, 1980), 2:695.

13. Philip Yancey, "Pitfalls of Christian Writing," in *Open Windows* (Westchester, Ill.: Crossway Books, 1982), 185.

14. Ann Japenga, "Pornography: Fuel for Rapists?", news article syndicated by the LA Times—Washington Post Service (31 January 1984). Japenga presents the research of UCLA professor Neil Malamuth and his surprising results.

15. This interpretation was first suggested to me by Donald Smith, Professor of World Mission at Western Conservative Baptist Seminary, Portland, Oregon.

The theme of this book is man's call to nobility and to rule as king. Cultural progress and scientific discovery, strength of character and nobility of mind, a refining of the spirit without a denial of the physical, a goal in eternity and a transfiguration of the world, all belong to his vocation as ruler.

His status as king must be seen in its context in the history of the universe. Behind all discord in nature lies a mighty revolution in the spirit-realm. If we are to understand the purpose and goal of man's creation, we must see them from the perspective of eternity before the universe and above all the earth came into being. From this standpoint we shall learn to see him as a kingly instrument in the hand of the Creator for the transfiguration of the world of nature. We shall see him also as a vessel for Divine grace and glory, called to worship, to conformity to God's image, to be a son of God through his creation, and to the vocation of ruler through eternity.

Erich Sauer
Foreword to *The King of the Earth*

Chapter 12

Being Human Indeed

*I*n the beginning of this book wc pointed to some of the societal ills that trouble us all. Many of these ills of contemporary culture are attacks upon our basic humanity. As we think about such new and heightened evils as abortion, pornography, child abuse, euthanasia, homosexuality, and the like, we sometimes get the feeling that they are all caused by a great conspiracy. That conspiracy is usually spoken of as "secular humanism."

Smoke-Filled Rooms

It would be an error, a grave error, to deny the reality or the pervasiveness of secularism in our age. Sometimes I get the feeling as I watch television that somewhere there is a group of malevolent men and women sitting in a smoke-filled room, leering at one another and asking, "Now that we have destroyed the American family, ridiculed the church, and undermined our military credibility, what can we attack next?" There may not be such a room of planners, but we all feel at times that there must be some collusion: Too many programs dealing with similar social issues group themselves on the pages of *TV Guide* to be merely an accident.

Numbers and Secrets

Yet we err if we speak of a massive humanist conspiracy. For one thing, the numbers of signers of the *Manifestos* is not high; second, secular humanists have been rather upfront in their proposals and plans.

When I speak of small numbers, I do not mean at all to minimize the risk. A small but highly active, intelligent, and dedicated cadre of secularists may be all that is needed to effect major continuing changes in our society. It took only one atheist to bring about significant shifts in public policy respecting prayer in the schools. A small group may be very dangerous indeed. But let's not magnify the problem by speaking of a "massive conspiracy," unless we gain better data than we presently have on the numbers.

The second reason that "massive conspiracy" is a faulty designation is that there does not seem to be all that much secrecy about this movement. The *Manifestos* have received wide publicity, and the publications of the secular humanists seem to have a sufficiently wide reading among fundamentalist and evangelical critics. If this is a conspiracy, the leaders have been rather inept in keeping their plans secret.

Evangelist for Secularism

One of the most prominent members of the secular humanist movement, and one of its most articulate spokesmen, is Paul Kurtz. Earlier we described Carl Sagan as an apostle of evolution; we may describe Kurtz as something of an evangelist for secularism. He is the former editor of the *Humanist,* is founding editor of *Free Inquiry,* has appeared on some sixty half-hour television programs advocating his point of view, and continues to teach philosophy at the State University of New York at Buffalo.

In a recent journal article, Paul Kurtz presents both his rebuttal of the well-known book by Tim LaHaye, *The Battle for the Mind,* as well as his action plan for secular humanism.[1] Kurtz describes (secular) humanism as the new scapegoat of the fundamentalist Right and then gives a point by point proposal for humanists to use in their desire for more prominence in

American life. This is not the mark of a conspiracy; it is rather an *agenda*. This article is available for all to read; it is not something that is being passed from principal to principal in our public schools, hidden within routine memos as a part of a surreptitious plot.

Should We Care?

Is secular humanism then something that the evangelical Christian ought to be concerned about? *Indeed it is.* Under the guise of pluralism, Kurtz and his associates advocate a frontal attack on biblical Christianity in all areas of the public sector in American life. Their approach to biblical faith is one of studied contempt. Here is a sampling of the disdain Kurtz shows for those who take biblical ideas seriously:

> To insist that all truths are in the Bible is pure nonsense and a throwback to an earlier age. We live in a highly sophisticated, technologically oriented, spaceage society. To think that the primitive doctrine of an ancient tribe of people on the shores of the Middle East can be applied in every case to our present problems stretches credulity. I don't see how such a view can, in the long run, prevail.[2]

In these arrogant words of contempt for Scripture, God, Israel, and the Christian faith, Kurtz clearly shows his colors. But note that fact: *He does show his colors.* Nothing is hidden; nothing is covert. His disdain for biblical faith is evident; his agenda for humanist victory is spelled out. He calls for the hard work of recruiting young humanist leaders, for humanist parents to raise their own children according to their own lights, and for their philosophical leaders to develop a morality based on rationalism (rather than revelation) that will be a compelling alternative for people in our brave new world.

Critical Balance

Rather than continuing to speak of a massive secular humanist conspiracy, let's deal with the matter as it is. As Carl F. H. Henry has noted, "We need a sense of critical balance.

Logically irreconcilable one liners may emulate Madison Avenue techniques, but they do little to serve either God's cause or our best evangelical interest."[3]

W. David Beck has presented this critical balance in a calm and thoughtful analysis of the grave dangers of secular humanism.[4] Beck, who holds the Ph.D. in philosophy from Boston University, argues that we need to face the principal ideas of secular humanism head on.

> In fact, this world view is riddled with contradictions and inadequacies, and we must force our society to see that, if we want to gain a real hearing. Secular humanism may not be an organization, but it is quite clear that for many it has ceased to be just a world view and has gained the status of a cause. It is obvious that Carl Sagan and Paul Kurtz, for example, are not dispassionate investigators searching for truth. They are preachers committed to communicating a message and convincing us of its truth.[5]

A Hodgepodge of Flaws

Beck then finds four fatal flaws in the system of secularism: (1) Secular humanism fails to account adequately for the origin of the universe; (2) it fails to account for the present order of things; (3) it is unable to provide an adequate basis for human morality; and (4) it contains a serious internal contradiction in that it posits a "natural universe," yet opts for "choice" in human behavior.[6] Some of these items are described by Henry as "a hodgepodge of illogical humanist dogma."[7]

So secularism does pose a real danger in our culture today. But we need to see that danger in context. As a matter of fact, some secularists are as concerned about certain societal ills as are many Christians. One of the most chilling analyses of the self-destructive bent of current technological culture is that of Ashley Montagu and Floyd Matson in their book, *The Dehumanization of Man*. It would be hard to find a more scathing indictment of the rampant immorality of our present age than in their chapter on the Playboy philosophy, "The Cheerful Robot and the Technocracy of Sex."[8]

An Alternative

What I have sought to present in this book is not so much an analysis of secular humanism as an alternative to it. The alternative is not a flight from humanism but a new orientation to the nature of being human. By "new" I do not mean that I have presented a discovery or an innovation; rather I have attempted to stress that which has been neglected but was there all the time. The new orientation is to see that *being truly human is basic to biblical Christianity*.

In our study of Psalm 8 we have seen that the question, "What is man?" is answered in a surprising way. Man is the apex of the creative works of God. As male and female, man was made in majesty to reflect the glory of God on earth. Man is the bearer of the very image of God; this is his differentia—that which marks him out from all other created things.

That which makes the presentation of humanism in Psalm 8 distinctive is that the nature of man is seen in the proper context of the praise of God. The Psalm begins and ends with the following frame:

O LORD, our Lord,
  how majestic is your name in all the earth!
                            (Psalm 8:1, 9)

These words envelop the doctrine of the majesty of man. They give man his perspective and his measure. When man is what he ought to be as male and female, then man brings new majesty to Yahweh his maker.

The Marvel of Being Human

The marvel of being man is that man may give praise to God. This is the point of verse 2:

From the lips of children and infants
  you have ordained praise. . . .

The smallest child is able to bring glory to highest God! And adults who maintain the childlike faith the Savior demands (Matthew 18:3) are able to magnify him to the heavens.

Man is never more man than when he is worshiping God!

On the basis of the central biblical doctrine of the Incarnation of the Savior Jesus, we may assert that in Christ there is the rediscovery of what it truly means to be human. What Adam was promised but lost, Jesus reclaims and bestows: *true humanity*. Only the Christian man or woman has the right to be called a humanist. The concept of a "secular" frame for humanism is an illusion. It is a deception of the first magnitude to speak of any humanism that is not in accord with being human in Christ.

Worship Together

Gordon Borror and I wrote together on the subject of corporate worship in our book, *Worship: Rediscovering the Missing Jewel*. Our principal concern was to bring new life and vitality to the worship patterns of evangelical churches. The emphasis in the Bible on worship is what we do *together*, for worship is a community act. A lone wolf in the life of faith is an anomaly. A solitary monk on a mountain peak is an aberration. One apart from the community of the worship of God is like a thirsty deer panting for refreshment (Psalm 42:1); when away from the place of worship we are prone to hang our harps in the bushes, laying aside all thoughts of music making (Psalm 137:2).

Nevertheless, the people who come to the assembly to worship God are those who are already worshiping God in the little moments of their daily lives. They are people who are experiencing their humanity in varied ways. They are people who, on hearing beautiful music, have their thoughts turn to the Lord of Song. They are people who, when they hear of human achievement, give praise to God for what man can do. They are people who, when they hear of human failure, reach out in compassion even as God has reached out to them. They are people who can read great books, enjoy great art, watch great plays— and in all, give great praise to God. These are a people who say *Yes* to life because they have said *Yes* to God.

Be Human

Let us therefore luxuriate in our humanity. God help us to become childlike (not childish) in developing again our sense of wonder. It was in wonder that we were made, and it is in wonder that we worship God. As we see the good and lovely things that man can do, let us praise God for this wonder. As we see the mystery and wonder in creation, let us praise God that we can participate in it.

Let us live life as God intended us to live it in the full enjoyment of our humanity. And let us learn our humanity from the Paragon of humanity, the Lord Jesus Christ. Only then will we know what it is to be fully and truly human. Only then will we be able to praise God for the majesty that is man.

Chapter 12, Notes

1. Paul Kurtz, "Defending Humanism Against Its Fundamentalist Critics," *Religious Humanism* 16 (Summer 1982): 102-12.

2. Ibid., 111.

3. Carl F. H. Henry, "Trumpeting God's Word to a Nation in Decision," in *The Christian Mindset in a Secular Society: Promoting Evangelical Renewal & National Righteousness* (Portland, Ore.: Multnomah Press, 1984), 10.

4. W. David Beck, "Secular Humanism: The Word of Man," in *Fundamentalist Journal* (November 1982):12-16. This is an article that should be reprinted and given wide coverage.

5. Ibid., 14.

6. Ibid., 14-15.

7. Henry, "Trumpeting God's Word," 14.

8. Ashley Montagu and Floyd Matson, *The Dehumanization of Man* (New York: McGraw-Hill, 1983), 24-56. This is a very hard-hitting book throughout.

Appendix

The Meaning of the Hebrew Verb Bara'

*T*he word *bara'* in and of itself does not speak of *creatio ex nihilo*. When one studies the extensive employment of this verb in the Hebrew Scripture, the parallel terms used with it, and the varied contexts in which it is found, the following conclusions may be made:

1. Whereas the word *bara'* may be used to describe an original creation out of nothing, there is nothing inherent in the word or in its usage to demand that such a concept is intended by the word. That is, if it was the intention of Moses to express the concept "creation out of nothing," he did not do so merely by the use of this verb. (To our knowledge, he had no single verb at hand to express this at all. No one word would have sufficed.)

2. The etymology of the verb *bara'*, while problematic, seems to suggest a basal meaning of shaping, fashioning, or building. Arguments based on etymology alone are always risky in language. We have been repeatedly warned concerning these risks, principally by Barr and Silva.[1] But there is no case to be made even from etymology for the supposed basic meaning of this verb as "creation out of nothing."

3. The usage of *bara'* in the Hebrew Bible (which, of course, is the determinant in understanding meaning), is

extensive with regard to things produced, is closely associated with a wide variety of synonyms of fashioning and making, often has about it the concept of newness, and—most notably—is used exclusively of the activity of God.

The Varied Uses of *Bara'*

Listed below are some of the types of uses of *bara'* in the Old Testament. As you survey this listing, allow it to enrich your perspective concerning the wonder of God's creative activity. Also ask how an awareness of the broad use of *bara'* may relate to its pronounced emphasis in the creation of man.

Here, then, are the principal uses of the verb *bara'*:

1. It is used of the creation of the universe:
   —the heavens and the earth (Genesis 1:1)
   —the ends of the earth (Isaiah 40:28)
   —the heavens (Isaiah 42:5; 45:18)
   —the north and the south (merism for the sum of creation; Psalm 89:12).
2. It is used of the elements of the universe:
   —the stars (Isaiah 40:26)
   —the wind (Amos 4:13).
3. It is used (surprisingly!) of the concepts of darkness and calamity (evil)—all things proceed from Yahweh the maker (Isaiah 45:7).
4. It is used of the nation of Israel, Yahweh's covenant people:
   —Jacob (Isaiah 43:1)
   —Israel (Isaiah 43:15).
5. It is used of the individual believing Jew:
   —the individual made in God's glory (Isaiah 43:7)
   —the individual man (Ecclesiastes 12:1).
6. It is used of the creatures of the sea and of the heavens (Genesis 1:21).
7. It is used of humanity:
   —man as male and female (Genesis 1:27; 5:1-2)

—man as human (Genesis 6:7; Deuteronomy
4:32; Isaiah 45:12).

8. It is used particularly of restorations and transfor-
mations:

—new heavens and new earth (Isaiah 65:17)

—coming of new salvation (Isaiah 45:8)

—"a new thing" (Jeremiah 31:22)

—Jerusalem as a rejoicing and his people as an
exultation (Isaiah 65:18)

—a clean heart (Psalm 51:10)

—a transformation of nature (Isaiah 41:20)

—a new thing in judgment (Numbers 16:30).

God's New Work

When we put all of these data together and compare and
contrast them, we may suggest that the consistent meaning of
the verb *bara'* is "to fashion anew—a divine activity."

Psalm 51:10, for example, is a text that is highly sugges-
tive for our study of the meaning of *bara'*. The reader should understand that the Hebrew word in parenthesis is not an inflected
term, but the basic form for purposes of identification.

Create (*bara'*) in me a pure heart, O God,
and renew a steadfast spirit within me.

These words of David the penitent suggest the central concept of
bara'. The verb speaks primarily of a divine act in refashioning.
If *bara'* says anything about material in creation, it speaks of renewal or refashioning. The parallel word "renew" is remarkable
in this verse. David's prayer is not that God would give him a
new heart and a new spirit "out of nothing," but that God would
restore to him the enjoyment of his salvation by renewing his
heart and spirit as a newly forgiven sinner. How far afield are the
common assumptions that the word itself means to make something out of nothing.

We will read two more texts in order to observe the varied
types of synonyms found with *bara'*. This is an important

element in gaining an understanding of Hebrew words because
of the parasynonymous dimension in the literature.

> It is I who made *('aśah)* the earth
> and created *(bara')* mankind upon it.
> My own hands stretched out *(naṭah)* the heavens;
> I marshaled *(ṣawah)* their starry hosts.
> (Isaiah 45:12)

> For this is what the LORD says—
> he who created *(bara')* the heavens,
> he is God;
> he who fashioned *(yaṣar)* and made *('aśah)* the earth,
> he founded *(kûn)* it;
> he did not create *(bara')* it to be empty,
> but formed *(yaṣar)* it to be inhabited—
> he says:
> "I am the LORD,
> and there is no other" (Isaiah 45:18).

Our Great God

As we read these verses in Isaiah we find that the verbs of
fashioning and making are used by this great poet to give an
impressive response to the work of God in creation. We may
further suggest that the verb *bara'* contributes significantly to a
major element in the creation text, that creation is a wonder that
calls for the adoration of God by his people. This is an important
emphasis of the German theologian Otto Procksch.[2]

Appendix, Notes
_____

1. James Barr, *The Semantics of Biblical Language* (Oxford: Oxford University Press, 1961); Moisés Silva, *Biblical Words and Their Meaning: An Introduction to Lexical Semantics* (Grand Rapids: Zondervan Publishing House, 1983), 35-51.

2. Otto Procksch, *Theology des Alten Testaments* (Gütersloh: C. Bertelsmann Verlag, 1950), 454-58.

A Bibliographic Guide for Further Reading

Select Books on the Nature of Man

Berkower, G. C. *Man: The Image of God,* in *Studies in Dogmatics.* Trans. by Dirk W. Jellema. Grand Rapids: Wm. B. Eerdmans Publishing Co., 1962. A standard work in the European Reformed tradition; subject of doctoral dissertation by Gerry Breshears of Western Conservative Baptist Seminary.

Kerkut, G. A. *The Implications of Evolution.* London: Pergamon Press, 1960. Stunning critique of standard evolutionary theory by a non-Christian evolutionist; professor of biochemistry and physiology, Southampton University, England.

Laidlaw, John. *The Biblical Doctrine of Man.* 1895. Reprint. Minneapolis: Klock & Klock, 1983. Reverent work; nineteenth-century classic.

Sauer, Erich. *The King of the Earth.* 1959. Reprint. Palm Springs, Calif.: Ronald N. Haynes, 1981. A biblical presentation of the nobility and royalty of man; theological and scientific interest throughout.

Smith, A. E. Wilder. *Man's Origin, Man's Destiny: A Critical Survey of the Principles of Evolution and Christianity.* Wheaton, Ill.: Harold Shaw, 1968. Award winning presentation of the case for biblical creation viewpoint; holder of three earned doctorates; professor of pharmacology at the Medical Center, University of Illinois.

Thielicke, Helmut. *Being Human . . . Becoming Human: An Essay in Christian Anthropology.* Trans. Geoffrey W. Bromiley. Garden City, N.Y.: Doubleday, 1984. Not light reading, but quite rewarding; renowned German theologian. Hats off to Dr. Bromiley (again!).

Select Books on Secular Humanism

Bayly, Joseph. *Winterflight.* Waco, Tex.: Word Books, 1981. An evangelical *1984;* novel depicting the societal consequences of secular humanism in the near future.

Geisler, Norman L. *Is Man the Measure? An Evaluation of Contemporary Humanism.* Grand Rapids: Baker Book House, 1983. Analysis of eight forms of contemporary humanism, with critical evaluation; by Professor of Systematic Theology, Dallas Theological Seminary.

Henry, Carl F. H. *The Christian Mindset in a Secular Society: Promoting Evangelical Renewal & National Righteousness.* Portland, Ore.: Multnomah Press, 1984. Vintage Henry; penetrating essays on public issues from a solid evangelical viewpoint.

Hitchcock, James. *What Is Secular Humanism: Why Humanism Became Secular and How It Is Changing Our World.* Ann Arbor, Mich.: Servant Books, 1982. Clear, readable guide; features vignettes of twenty-one figures in the development of humanism.

Montagu, Ashley and Floyd Matson. *The Dehumanization of Man.* New York: McGraw-Hill Book Co., 1983. Strong critique of dehumanizing elements in Western society; not from a Christian viewpoint.

Sagan, Carl. *Cosmos.* New York: Random House, 1980. A beautifully produced book presenting religious secularism by the "apostle of evolution."

Webber, Robert E. *Secular Humanism: Threat and Challenge.* Grand Rapids: Zondervan Publishing House, 1982. Brief, balanced, to the point.

Select Books on Being Human

Allen, Ronald Barclay. *Praise! A Matter of Life and Breath.* Nashville, Tenn.: Thomas Nelson, 1980. Introduction to the reading of the Psalms, centering in the notion of praise.

Allen, Ronald B. and Gordon L. Borror. *Worship: Rediscovering the Missing Jewel.* Portland, Ore.: Multnomah Press, 1982. Companion to the present volume, centering on the renewal of worship in the evangelical church.

Gundry, Patricia. *Heirs Together.* Grand Rapids: Zondervan Publishing House, 1980. A splendid case for mutuality in Christian marriage.

Howard, Thomas. *Hallowed Be This House.* Wheaton, Ill.: Harold Shaw, 1979. Learning to see the sacred in everyday living.

Packer, J. I. and Thomas Howard. *Christianity: The True Humanism.* Waco, Tex.: Word Books, 1984. A warmly anticipated volume by two award winning evangelical authors.

Peterson, Eugene H. *Run with the Horses: The Quest for Life at Its Best.* Downers Grove, Ill.: InterVarsity Press, 1983. Reflections on the Book of Jeremiah, creatively presented for enrichment of life today.

Rookmaaker, H. R. *The Creative Gift: Essays on Art and the Christian Life.* Westchester, Ill.: Cornerstone Books, 1981. Learning to think Christianly concerning art.

Ryken, Leland. *Triumphs of the Imagination: Literature in Christian Perspective.* Downers Grove, Ill.: InterVarsity Press, 1979. Excellent guide to learn to think Christianly about world literature; will help you to break the shackles of Tertullian.

Smith, Jane Stuart and Betty Carlson. *A Gift of Music: Great Composers and Their Music.* Westchester, Ill.: Crossway Books, 1983. A Christian listener's guide to great music; open at random and enjoy!

Sproul, R. C. *In Search of Dignity*. Ventura, Calif.: Regal Books, 1983. Learning to appreciate the worth of each individual, an essential element in learning to be truly human.

Wilson, Earl D. *Loving Enough to Care*. Portland, Ore.: Multnomah Press, 1984. The cover says this book could change your life—this is not hype.

Select Books about Those Who Are Truly Human

Monty, Shirlee. *May's Boy: An Incredible Story of Love*. Nashville, Tenn.: Thomas Nelson, 1981. May Lemke's triumph as one who is truly human; the miracle of Leslie Lemke, a nearly discarded genius.

Nason, Diane with Birdie Etchison. *The Celebration Family*. Nashville, Tenn.: Thomas Nelson, 1984. A family in Sisters, Oregon, that has enough love to keep growing at thirty!

Scripture Index

Subject Index

Abortion, 11, 19
  and experiments, 20
  and murder, 49
  rights of women in, 41
Absurdist view of man, 38
Action coalitions, 40-41
Adam, 129n
Agur, 141
Albright, William Foxwell, 59
Alexander, Myrna, 48
Allen, Ronald B., 52n, 93n, 94n,
  109n, 129n, 170n, 191n, 192n
Angels, 71
Antichrist, 118
Anti-Semitism, 49, 188
Antitype, 164
Arian-Athanasian controversy, 165,
  170n
Augustine, 122

Baal, 60-61
Baer, Richard A., Jr., 150n
Bainton, Roland H., 34
Baker, Russell, 178, 191n
Balance, 40-41, 114-19, 175, 197-98
Bara', 84-85, 93n, 163, 203-6
  not *creatio ex nihilo*, 203
  to fashion anew, 205
  synonyms of, 206
  and wonder, 206
Barr, James, 203, 206n
Bayly, Joseph, 20-21, 22n
Beck, W. David, 198, 201n
Being and meaning, 25
Berkouwer, G. C., 109n
Bible and science, 42-43
  See also Creation
Biblical humanism
  and balance, 173-76
  body in, 177-78
  and Christianity, 199
  culture and, 174
  and dignity of man, 61

  emotions in, 178-79
  and image of God, 93
  and Jesus as Son of Man, 128-29
  luxuriate in, 201
  and mission, 190-91
  and music, 179-81
  and nature, 183-85
  and others, 188-89
  and praise of God, 13, 199-200
  and science, 181-83
  and self, 176
  and things, 185-88
  and God's wisdom, 169
  wonder in, 201
  and women, 189-90
  not worm, 51
  and worship, 200-1
Bloesch, Donald G., 109n, 134
Boice, James Montgomery, 22n,
  34n, 109n
Bonhoeffer, Dietrich, 85, 94n
Borror, Gordon, 93n, 200
Bow hunt, 184
Bradley, Walter L., 42-43, 52n
Bromiley, Geoffrey W., 128, 130n
Brown, Harold O. J., 115, 129
Brownlee, Shannon, 150n
Bruder, Judith, 96, 97, 109n
Buechner, Frederick, 80, 81, 177
Bultmann, Rudolf, 29-31, 34n
Burns, George, 33, 34n
Bury, J. B., 64n
Bush, Frederic William, 150n

Cain, and sin's desire, 146
Camus, Albert, 38, 52n
Canaan, religion of, 59-60
Capital punishment, 105
Cassuto, Umberto, 84, 93n, 94n,
  150n
Change in standards, 18, 25, 39-40
  See also Societal ills
Chariots of Fire, 169, 178